Becoming a Mother on Fire

A personal coach for mothers! I loved it. What a great idea. Garber really explains the pulls and demands we feel as moms. This book is all about fulfilling your own potential while supporting your children to do the same. Moms need this book!

– Jennifer Garner, actress, producer, mother of two, Los Angeles

Wonderful strategies for taking care of yourself while trying to take care of everybody else. Moms will love this message: You can be a great mom AND still have a life!

– Amy Sky, award-winning songwriter, singer, producer, mental health advocate, and mother of two, www.amysky.com, Toronto

MOTHERS … This is your chance to find yourself again! Garber's coaching is powerful in this book. She will take you by the hand and guide you easily from making a commitment to yourself to creating a better life for you and your family. After applying Lisa's discoveries to your own life, you will be much more powerful as a woman and mother. I highly recommend this book for any mother wanting to regain her sense of self and connect with why she matters to the world.

– Deborah R. Monroe, Ignite Achievements Int'l Inc.,
MA, Master EQ Practitioner, Organizational
Development and Coaching, San Antonio

I plan to recommend this book to my clients. A divorce can really shake a mother's identity and make her question herself. And of course, because she is so concerned about her children getting through it, she can forget about herself. But no more! This book gives a mother permission to focus some attention on herself so she can take that journey toward creating a better life for herself and her children.

– Nicola Savin, family law lawyer and partner,
Birenbaum Steinberg Landau Savin & Colraine, Toronto

The coaching process in this book has the power to change mothers' lives, just as it did mine. I especially love the chapter on setting Wildly Audacious Goals (WAGs). I started coaching with Lisa when I was a new mother. It helped me to step outside my comfort zone. It wasn't easy but I began an in-depth path of self-discovery that continues to result in positive changes in my life even today. Now I work in a career I love, live in my dream home, and find myself surrounded by energetic, successful people. Most importantly, I am more connected to my own children, and those I love. I celebrate what I call "mini miracles" in my life that keep me inspired, and never cease to amaze me. For all busy moms, if you have an open mind, and are willing to do your own inner work, this book makes for a transformational journey. Go for it!

– Carolyn Hidalgo, Professional Life Coach, CA, CPCC, Co-Founder of Focused Energy Inc., mother of three including twins, Toronto

Congratulations Lisa. As a woman and children's health specialist with 25 years of experience in the field, I congratulate you on your book and your program. As well, having been part of your first coaching group for ten years I can speak to your words and wisdom with confidence and conviction. Women must hang on to themselves in order to be the best parent and person they can be. Your program is a wonderful tool to help them do just that!

– Jan Andrews RN, BScN, MN, mother of three, Oakville, Canada

REALLY knowing and understanding my core values, allowed me to find meaning in my new role as a mom. The realization that the source of my unhappiness stemmed from not living an "authentic" life made a huge and positive impact in every aspect of my life. The Mothers on Fire Coaching Program™ in this book was pivotal in my journey to becoming a better mom and a happier, more complete "me."

– Claudia Gonzalez, MBA, mother of two, Australia

First and foremost, wow! "Fulfilling the longing of your soul"—
that line makes me want to cry. It's so powerful, so magical ... love it!
I will CONFIDENTLY *and* PROUDLY *share this with any mom I know.*

– Grace Y. Attard, creator of The e-Spot™ and enSpire
Coaching Inc. and a Mother on Fire, www.e-spot.ca
and www.enspirecoaching.com, Oakville, Canada

This book is valuable for all women in any stage of life—not only
mothers. I recognize both myself and clients in many of the descrip-
tions in these pages. The tug of loyalties women experience is universal.
If you feel caught between your partner and your girlfriends, your
work and personal life balance, or between your growing kids and
your aging parents, this book can offer you helpful insights. Lisa
provides readers with valuable tools used by professional coaches to
reclaim their birthright—to be an empowered, joyful and fulfilled
human being—by "coaching themselves" step by step through these
practical exercises. I wish this book had been around years ago!

– Joni Mar, CPCC, MCC, Master Certified Coach,
www.jonimar.com, Vancouver

Mothers are also birthed at the same time as their baby. One thing
I tell my clients is that transition is scary. When we are in transition
we are neither here nor there. This book has valuable insights and
exercises to help moms going through the transition to become the
mother they truly are inside.

– Owen Williams, author, *The Relationship Revolution,*
executive, life and relationship coach,
www.relationshipexcellence.com, Toronto

Garber has done a beautiful job of making a complex subject
accessible and easy to read. The self-exploration in the coaching
exercises has the potential for a mother to transform her life. I wish I
had this book when I was the young mother of a wild and crazy kid!

– Tzabia Siegel, BAPhEd, CHN and mother,
www.weightlesscreativity.com, Toronto

BECOMING A MOTHER ON FIRE

*A Guide to Being a Mom
Without Losing Yourself*

LISA GARBER, M.ED., CPCC

Mothers on Fire Inc.
Toronto, Canada

Mothers on Fire Inc.
260 Adelaide St. E, Suite 217
Toronto, ON M5A 1N1
Canada
e-mail: contactus@mothersonfire.com

Book design by Sara Patton
Printed in Canada

ISBN 978-0-9685596-1-1

The names and details of the coaching examples provided in this book
have been changed when necessary to respect the confidentiality of the
coaching relationship.

The information in this book is not intended to replace the services of a
health care professional. Please consult your doctor if you show signs of
depression or other emotional distress. Please know, you are not alone,
and your doctor can help.

*This book is dedicated to my aunt and uncle
Grace and Malcolm Garber,
who gave me a home to both
heal my heart and pursue my dreams.*

CONTENTS

Chapter 7   Making Sure Your Inner Fire Expresses Your Authentic Self

FOREWORD

We are so excited to be able to write this foreword for our friend, coach, and partner, Lisa Garber. Many years have passed since we first met Lisa at an introductory life-coaching meeting. We heard her speak about fulfilling ourselves, living our dreams and planning the life we really wanted. It all sounded great, yet almost impossible to imagine. After all, we were mothers. We got excited about our children's and spouses' dreams. Our fulfillment would come later—perhaps when the kids were in school.

We had both left successful careers to stay at home with our children. We wanted to do that. We still do. But pretty quickly we learned how motherhood could be both rewarding and challenging. It can make you want to scream from frustration and weep from feelings of love and responsibility you never thought were possible. Motherhood is such a powerful experience that it can engulf you. You stop doing a hobby that you used to love. You stop connecting with some friends because there is no time. You feel guilty about so much. Your hair, your clothes, your priorities, your life—you cannot believe how it all has changed so dramatically. There is joy for sure. But there is grief too for the loss of the life and freedom you once had.

Life coaching was our wake-up call. It allowed us to go deep within ourselves and truly listen to our hearts. We were able to be honest and share with the other members of our life-coaching group that something was missing in our lives. We were a little lost. We were relieved to learn that we were not alone. So many other moms were feeling that way too. Lisa somehow made us feel okay about facing this truth. It didn't mean we were bad mothers. She helped us realize that a life with more happiness, fulfillment, and passion was the one we could create for ourselves right now. She showed us the road and gently pushed and guided us down it.

What an incredible journey it has been and continues to be! Except for the fact that our children are older and that we have more of them, our outer circumstances look pretty much the same as the day we started coaching. Yet, something is profoundly different. We are different. Baby step by baby step, we rediscovered our dreams and desires. We found ourselves again. We no longer believe that guilt has to be part of the job. Our true and complete selves didn't have to disappear because we had children to take care of. We connected with things that really excited us and made us feel alive. Today, we are committed to bringing more of that aliveness and joy into our lives. We have stopped waiting for the perfect time; instead we just do it. We have become Mothers on Fire!

It is with deep joy and love that we invite you along this

path too. Lisa has written this book as a guide for you to follow. You will feel her gentle guidance all the way through, as if she is sitting across from you, giving you her alternative perspective. You will be guided by her expertise, entertained by her wit and enlightened by her wisdom. She will shine a light on the possibilities for your life just as she did for us. We hear her voice in our heads all the time. *Okay, so you can't do everything you wanted—what* can *you do?*

In these pages, you will feel Lisa's passion for helping mothers live happier lives.

We are still at home with our children, living extremely busy lives and feeling the weight of responsibility of motherhood. Some of it we love. Some of it we are still trying to transform. The difference is, we make *ourselves* a priority too. We nurture our family and also nurture ourselves. We are pursuing our wildest dreams. The biggest one was starting our company, Mothers on Fire Inc. (www.mothersonfire.com).

Mothers on Fire Inc. is about living with energy, passion, and, most of all, inner fire. It's about finding your authentic self and loving who you are. Deep down, we feel more complete, enriched, and at peace. We believe mothers all over the world can feel this way. This is the book we all wished we'd had when we became mothers.

So, forget about the dishes in the sink and the closet you've been meaning to organize. Sit down and enjoy this book. Let yourself feel hopeful, knowing that you can create a happier life even though it might look different from your old life or from how you expected your new life to be. We feel blessed and grateful to be able to share our story and this book with you.

Renée Walker
Sandra De Tina
Oakville, Canada
June 2009

In all my years of both counseling and coaching, I have seen this one truth over and over again—of all the things we think children need, what they need the most is their mother to be happy.

—Lisa Garber, author and life coach

INTRODUCTION

If the world seems cold to you,
kindle fires to warm it.

—Lucy Larcom, poet

Hello. *How are you?*
Fine.
No, really. How are you?

How are you?—such a common question—most of us just discard it with a flippant answer. *Fine* might work for others, but I am a life coach and psychotherapist. I don't actually want the quick and easy version. I don't want the answer you give to acquaintances or other moms down the street. I am not asking this question to be polite. I am asking you this question because I really want to know the answer.

So, please tell me honestly.

Are you living out of the longing of your soul?

Hold on, I just heard you say. *Where did that come from? Living out of the longing of my soul? Isn't that a completely different question than how am I?*

It may look that way at first. So let me explain. You know how some people, maybe someone you've heard about in the news or read about in magazines, seem to live from a deep excitement within them? You know, like the guests you see on *Oprah* who seem to know exactly who they are, go after what they want and, as a result, have a passion for their lives that just pours out of them?

Well, I don't believe that living a full and passionate life is reserved for just a chosen few. I believe that we can all live like that. If those few can have it, it is available for all of us. It means, however, that we have to take a risk and start to look within ourselves to those simmering embers of desire buried under years of roles, responsibilities, and doing the "proper" things. It means doing the work to find and then honor our authentic self. Connection to our true self is an important component to living a complete and passionate life.

Your authentic self wants out. It is pushing to come out. Those deeply buried desires that we have shelved or put on hold—those are the longing of your soul.

Most mothers are not connected to that longing anymore. Too many live vicariously through others. When we first start working together, their lives are narrowly focused on their children and on being the best mom in the world, at the expense of some of their souls' other desires.

Motherhood has extraordinary challenges. First, you have given your body and then your instincts may be telling you to give your soul. Your life has shifted from taking care of yourself to feeling deeply responsible for the life of another. People are not kidding when they say that becoming a parent is life changing. Having such a profound shift in priorities is natural for mothers.

Some mothers are able to make the shift in stride. But many of my clients are thrust into motherhood without a road map for the emotional upheaval they experience. They have had an expectation that life was to be "totally fulfilling" after motherhood—which it can be for some, but, so many others feel that even with the moments of joy that come in motherhood, there is something else missing. They often do not feel happy. My clients describe it as a longing for something more. I describe it as the longing of your soul.

Something is missing for many moms.

In my practice, I have seen that most mothers are prepared intellectually for the day-to-day work of being a mother. But, they are seldom prepared for the deep bond of love and attachment they experience. As a result, their outlook becomes narrower and narrower as the baby seems to take over their time, focus, heart, mind, and soul.

It is like having an all-consuming love affair with a boyfriend. Remember? Perhaps you've experienced this, or had a friend like this. All of a sudden her interests have changed to match his. She doesn't hang out with you and your friends anymore. And when you finally get a chance to spend time with her, all she can talk about is him!

Oh, yes. Love can consume us. And the powerful love of a mother for her children is no exception. If mothers are not careful, they can lose themselves in motherhood. And that's what's missing for the moms I coach. What's missing is you!

A mother's focus can become too narrow.
Somehow it has become the norm for motherhood to be so child-centric that it is robbing women of their identities. Loving their kids has started to mean losing themselves. They are so over-identified with being a "mom" that everything else they were before they had babies fades into the background and disappears. In addition, they are so careful to make everyone else happy that they have forgotten how to make themselves happy. They lose sight of what they want as the longing of their soul gets buried.

When a mother, looking for something more, goes out to find support, she often runs into a dilemma. Most of the products and literature aimed at mothers seem to recognize them as mothers only and neglect them as individuals. On the other hand, most personal development methods focus only on the individual and therefore can ignore the reality of what it's like to be a mother. This book is intended to bridge that gap.

THE MOTHERS ON FIRE COACHING PROGRAM™

The truth is, I have met a lot of moms who were just not that happy, didn't know what to do about it, and were afraid to admit it. So, in 1997, I started a life-coaching group for mothers. That's right. Just like an athlete who wants to go for an Olympic gold medal seeks out someone to help her, a mother looking to improve the quality of her life would seek me out. The exercises, stories, and ideas in this book are all based on the work I have done with the many mothers I have coached over the years both in groups and one-on-one.

Coaching, in general, is a conversation with a purpose. Its purpose is to support you in creating the life you truly *want*, and not the one you or someone else thinks you *should* be living. In contrast to traditional psychotherapy, which focuses on healing traumas or dysfunction, life coaching looks forward towards goals and dreams. Life coaching doesn't talk about fixing things as much as it talks about discovering your authentic self and living from it. And that is what it means to be complete and on fire.

A coaching conversation is about deep and meaningful topics. For example, in this book we will talk about making a commitment to yourself, reconnecting with your emotions and needs, finding your authentic self, and setting goals that will honor the longing of your soul. We will also talk about strategies and tools to help get the results you really want.

I will not be focusing on giving you advice, doing therapy, or mentoring you. All those activities might have a coaching component in them, but pure coaching is all about helping you to find your own answers, the ones that are within you. The Mothers on Fire Coaching Program™ in this book will point you in the direction of your authentic self. It will lead you to your very own unique vein of gold and then help you to mine it.

The main tool in this book is the series of empowering

questions. These questions will encourage you to look deep within yourself. They might ask you to question your assumptions. They will certainly help you to discover yourself in ways that can be hard to do on your own.

By the way, you have already experienced an empowering question. Remember when I asked you if you were living out of the longing of your soul? That is an empowering question.

Why the metaphor of fire?

In 2007, I joined forces with two of my life-coaching graduates and we built a web-based business called Mothers on Fire. *On fire*—that is how my partners Renée Walker and Sandra De Tina felt after their years of coaching.

Fire is a universal symbol for transformation. The great mythological bird the Phoenix rises from the ashes of a fire. Wizards are said to use fire to transform base metals into gold. The Yogis of India wear saffron-colored robes as a symbol of the metaphorical fire that burns away their earthly bonds and liberates them.

Fire is also a symbol for passion. It is those deep desires that are burning to be realized. It is energy that longs to live and express itself.

Fire is life. If you were stranded on an island, making a fire would be your first priority. It allows you to boil water and send up a rescue signal. Fire keeps you warm and protects you from animals.

But, fire is also risky. It is unpredictable. As well as preserving life, it can take it away. It can be scary when it is out of control.

Indeed, fire is powerful. In Greek mythology, Prometheus was punished for eternity by the gods for bringing fire to humans. The gods saw it as giving humans too much power, something they wanted to keep for themselves.

Renée and Sandra were passionate about helping other mothers feel powerful, find themselves, and feel the happiness and passion that they had found from coaching. That is how they came up with the name—Mothers on Fire. When a mother works through the Mothers on Fire Coaching Program™, she discovers her inner passion, her inner flame, her more powerful and real self. She is ready and willing to take the risks inherent in change in order to reap the rewards. She knows growth is a part of life—a rich, rewarding and fulfilling life, one that touches many people in positive ways. She wants to live life to its fullest and not waste a drop of it.

Life coaching will benefit you and your family.

When I first started coaching mothers, I was really impressed by their commitment to their children and to their families in general. Their commitment was so deep that they were leery about what this life coaching was all about and made it clear that they would not be interested in anything that could jeopardize their families' happiness or stability.

Are you wondering about that, too? I want to assure you that the Mothers on Fire Coaching Program™ is not about taking anything away from motherhood. Is that a relief? You can take a deep breath now and relax. Rather than compromising your role as a mother, the processes and exercises in this book are about bringing your best self to motherhood, a more authentic and complete you. It is about fulfilling yourself as an individual, a whole person. That includes being a mother, but it also includes many other things as well. It is about recognizing that your role and job as a mother is one part of who you are. You are a mom AND so much more.

You are a mom AND so much more.

I have capitalized the word "AND" because most moms tend to put a "BUT" in sentences like that one. They might say: "I would love to get back to my painting, BUT I'm a mom first and that's that." Or: "I used to love working out at the gym, BUT I'm a mom now and my children's activities come first." Have you ever thought: "I find myself wanting more or wishing for something that will be more stimulating and satisfying, BUT I'm a mom now and my children have to be my focus no matter how I feel"? You might even be feeling fulfilled as a mother, BUT not finding time for your friends, or noticing that you feel angry and frustrated too much.

I can always tell in conversations with moms when there is a big "BUT" coming. So I will tell you here what I tell them in person: There is more for you, if that is what you need and want. There is more for you AND you can have it. You get to be a great mom AND still pursue other things that are meaningful to you. You get to fulfill yourself and feel complete while you are helping your family fulfill themselves. It doesn't have to be one or the other. In fact, you will probably find that the more fulfilled you are, the more enriched your family life becomes.

Your complete life is the goal.

Having you live a complete and fulfilled life is the goal of the Mothers on Fire Coaching Program™. What does that mean? A complete life means

- achieving balance by not living in the extremes, but finding the middle ground

- living your life with purpose by connecting with your feelings, needs, and core values

- working out your priorities and being at peace with them

- attaining your goals

- reducing your stress by taking care of yourself

- finding things you feel passionate about and giving them a place in your life

- feeling fulfilled within

- staying connected to the person you were before becoming a mother

- feeling like a Mother on Fire

It can feel like a daunting task, living a complete life, but what will it feel like if you don't try? What will happen in the next year, two years, or five years if you don't make some changes in yourself and in your life? Are you comfortable with the answer?

Now let yourself imagine it is a year from now and you have put in the time and the effort and made some great discoveries and changes. How will you feel then?

It's up to you. It is your choice as to how you want to feel. Like Dorothy in *The Wizard of Oz*, you have always had the power to go home. You and only you can make that choice to fulfill yourself and feel more complete.

How to Use This Book

I want this book to open up your eyes, your ears, your heart, and your mind to the possibilities for your life. The first part will give you some background and theory on the problem mothers have of losing themselves in motherhood. You will look at the ten characteristics of a Mother on Fire and how to overcome the obstacles to change. In Part Two, you will start the Mothers on Fire Coaching Program™. You will learn about the six steps you can take to build the inner fire that is the expression of your true self, the fire that represents a complete and fulfilled life.

In Step One of the program, you will make a powerful and determined decision to become a Mother on Fire. That decision will provide the momentum you need as you progress through the exercises in the program. Step Two is where you will survey the territory of your current life and take stock. Your inner fire must be built within it currently, and not some time in the future. Step Three will give you a new perspective on your emotions and needs. You will spark your inner fire with the energy that comes from connecting with your feelings and meeting your own needs. In Step Four, you will discover your core values. Your authentic self lives here, in the honoring of those values. You want to make sure your inner fire is an expression of your true self. By Step Five you are ready to set some goals—but not just any goals. These are the goals that will lead you straight to the fulfillment of your authentic self and a complete life. These goals are the branches that will fuel your inner fire. And finally, Step Six, the last step is where you find your passion, reconnect to the longing of your soul and become a Mother on Fire.

Part Three talks about a new beginning and how you can keep your inner flame burning brightly.

I, and my partners Renée and Sandra, want you to receive as much value as possible from reading this book. Perhaps it will be a new perspective on some aspect of your life, perhaps it will be a reconnection with a passion you've had for a long time but have been putting aside. Whatever it is, give yourself a chance to take your life to another level. You will always be grateful that you did.

Just as a caution, it's good to realize that real, lasting change happens over time. It is not about a quick fix. This book is a workbook. That means there is work to be done. You may want to read it straight through at first to get an overview. But I hope you will do more than that. Your vitality and commitment will make this program work for you. A well-used workbook will be frayed at the edges, highlighted here and there, marked with notes scribbled in the margins. I also recommend you get a journal to use for writing out the exercises. The two together can become a living document that records your story, your changes, your journey to fulfillment.

In addition to this book, Mothers on Fire has an exciting, information-packed website for you to use as a powerful resource on your journey. You will find articles, exercises, blogs, and forums where you can join other moms who are working through the exercises in this book. The website is at www.mothersonfire.com. You can also sign up for our free ezine and other fun resources. The site is always changing, so come and visit us often. We want to hear about your journey to becoming a Mother on Fire.

LETTING YOUR INNER LIGHT SHINE

Underlying this book and all our work at Mothers on Fire is our deep conviction that the world needs your light, your voice, and your full participation. When I think of you and so many moms I have worked with, I think about Marianne Williamson's inspirational words from her book *A Return to Love: Reflections on the Principles of A Course in Miracles*:

> *Our deepest fear is not that we are inadequate. Our deepest fear is that we are powerful beyond measure. It is our light, not our darkness that most frightens us. We ask ourselves, who am I to be brilliant, gorgeous,*

talented, fabulous? Actually, who are you not to be?
You are a child of God. Your playing small does not
serve the world. There is nothing enlightened about
shrinking so that other people won't feel insecure
around you. We are all meant to shine, as children do.
We were born to make manifest the glory of God that
is within us. It's not just in some of us; it's in everyone.
And as we let our own light shine, we unconsciously
give other people permission to do the same. As we are
liberated from our own fear, our presence automati-
cally liberates others.

Doesn't every mother want her children to shine? Doesn't every mother want her children to be the best they can be? Well, it starts with you. Not just your parenting skills. I mean it starts with you allowing your inner light to shine, your inner passion to be expressed, your inner fire to burn brightly. The greatest gift you can ever give to your children is for you to live a rich and passionate life. In that way, you free them to do the same.

So, it's time to jump in. Remember this: growth is messy. No one does it perfectly, and perfection should not be a goal. No two people do it the same way. And no one knows how long it will take. Give yourself permission to make mistakes, try again, and enjoy the process. Oh, and give yourself permission to succeed also.

I recommend you take baby steps with your personal growth. Refrain from any urge to attach unrealistic expectations on yourself as you go through this process. Perfectionism will stop you before you even start. By doing whatever you can do in a slow and consistent way, one day you will turn around and realize how far you have come. You will recognize this realization because you will be experiencing more and more moments of joy in your life, every day.

You can change your life.

So, are you ready? It's time to wake up your inner flame so you can become a Mother on Fire. Let's glow, girl!

PART ONE

MOTHERS ON FIRE AND YOU

1

MOTHERS HAVE
LOST THEMSELVES

*The greatest gift you can give to your children
is to live a rich, passionate, and complete life.
In that way, you free them to do the same.*

In any relationship based on love, whether it is the bond of mother and child, marriage, family, or friendship, it is extremely important to maintain your sense of self. Otherwise, relationships can begin to break down. Good relationships depend on some space for strength. Loving others, even deeply and profoundly, does not mean losing yourself in that love. Actually, it can, and hopefully will mean becoming more and more yourself. It is in that space that we all can breathe and grow. Otherwise, like a too-tightly planted grove of trees, we can suffocate at our roots and begin to fade away.

Finding that breathing space is a great challenge for mothers. This is true not only when the child is an infant. If a mother doesn't work on maintaining her sense of self as the child grows, the attachment between a mother and her infant can lead to over-identification, over-achievement, and over-dependence on both sides. A mother's sense of self-worth and self-esteem can become inextricably linked with how well her child performs in life. With this, the mother can become less and less involved in her own life and over-involved in her children's lives. The mother's personal power is diminished. Without even realizing it, she has lost herself.

FOUR WAYS MOTHERS LOSE THEMSELVES

1. Self-sacrifice

Putting family first and themselves last—or even not at all— is a behavior I see a lot with mothers. The drive to sacrifice oneself originates in our instincts. Mothers have a primal urge to protect their young; it is a powerful survival instinct. But there are other influences also. There are the stereotypical ideals of what a mother *should* be, as portrayed in our media. There is our own early childhood learning. There are pressures from today's philosophies of parenting, which can be hard to keep up with! A lot of these philosophies seem to put children's wants, needs, and lives before their parents'. In addition, mothers receive a barrage of advice every day from their own families, peers, doctors, and so on.

Mothers have been conditioned to believe that motherhood and sacrifice are one and the same. Many of my clients have given up their individual dreams and become almost totally consumed by raising their children. Instead of fitting their children around their lives, moms today are fitting their lives around their children. Is it any wonder that so many moms are unhappy?

There are many ways to be a great mother.
It is important for mothers to understand that there are many
ways to be a great mother and do a great job as a parent.
Recognizing that you do not have to sacrifice your talents,
self-care, dreams, plans, passions, personal needs—namely,
your life and yourself—to be a good enough mother is a great
place to start breaking the cycle of self-sacrifice.

This is a hard concept for many of my clients to understand, or accept. In the beginning of our coaching sessions,
often my clients are just not able to see another way. A mother's
first priority is doing what's best for her child, naturally. But,
through the coaching process, as a mother starts to reconnect
with her own personal wants and needs, a light goes on and
she realizes that having a more complete life might in fact be
in the best interest of her children. She starts to change and
accept that she can reconnect with her self, and bring her life
and parenting style back into balance without damaging her
children.

**Self-sacrificing is not necessarily in the best interest of
your children.**
Sacrificing your own needs and wants for the sake of your
children can actually backfire on a well-meaning mother. I
have seen in my practice women who felt held back by their
own mother's self-sacrifice. Rather than feeling free to pursue
their own dreams, they felt guilty if they did not sacrifice for
their children the same way their mothers did. In addition,
they felt and continue to feel an overwhelming obligation

to their own mothers. It is almost like survivor's guilt—as if they are saying, "I can't have a personally fulfilling life if you didn't."

Self-sacrifice can backfire in other ways, too. For example, by making the fulfillment of your child's every need the center of your family life, you could be teaching them a lesson of self-centeredness. Children are self-centered by nature—they have to learn to see from another's perspective. They have to be taught that others have needs also and that they need to learn to respect that.

Not only do children need to learn not to be self-centered, they also need to learn confidence, self-reliance, and self-esteem from somewhere, too, so that they can grow up to follow their own dreams. If their closest role models are not sending empowering messages through their own actions, who will? As you start to live a more complete life by following some of your dreams and interests outside of your role as a mother, you will be setting a good example.

But, above all else, isn't it just better for your children to have a mother who is satisfied, happy, relaxed, and feels good about herself? When you are stressed or don't feel personally fulfilled, when your life is focused on meeting everyone else's needs but your own, you are more likely to have difficulty in all your relationships.

Your rich and passionate life matters.
Feeling more complete matters. It matters to you and to everyone you touch and are touched by. Your spark and your

happiness contribute to the joy and well-being of everyone. You know what they say: "When mama's happy, everyone's happy." You've probably seen that a million times in other people's lives, but it can be hard to see it in your own.

Living out of the longing of your soul is one of the best things you can do for your children because when you work at reconnecting with and fulfilling yourself, not just as a mother, but as a whole person, it gives your children permission to do the same. It is like giving them a passport to a great adventurous life, stamped by your modeling and fueled by your joy.

2. Over-functioning

One of my coaching clients used to wear me out when she would check in at the beginning of our group coaching meetings. I could not believe what she did in a day, a week, a month! As a stay-at-home mom with three children and a husband who worked long hours, she did everything for everybody. I really mean *everything* and *everybody*. And she had to do it all perfectly. She was totally stressed out and thought it was normal.

Isn't this the way it has to be? she asked, incredulous at my suggestion that she might be over-functioning.

All of the other members in the coaching group agreed with her.

This is just how it is for moms, someone said. *You don't understand.*

Au contraire! I do understand. I too was a classic "over-functioner" when it came to my husband and step-kids. But, because of my own personal development work, I learned that my over-functioning was really over-compensating. I was a human *doing* because my human *being* felt empty. All that "doing" was a fantastic distraction from the quiet but insistent longing of my soul, a longing that I was too afraid to really listen to, a longing that pointed to my need for creative expression and a more spiritual life. Over-functioning is a great way to avoid dealing with any emptiness we might be feeling within, an emptiness that seems much too scary to pay attention to for fear it might rock the boat.

The fear of rocking the boat stems from "all or nothing" thinking. Our thoughts scare us. We have an irrational fear that if we begin to make changes, we will ultimately have to change everything. We are afraid that if we look too closely, the small problems in our marriage, for example, may turn out to be really big ones. We fear that the anger and frustration we sometimes feel towards our children means we are terrible mothers. We might even worry that the emptiness we sense within might turn out to be a giant void that could only be filled by chucking everything and becoming a missionary in Africa!

I hope you are smiling a little when you read this. It is natural to have some fear about rocking the boat when, as mothers, we are focused on providing a safe and secure home for our children. It is when it escalates into "all or nothing" thinking that our fears become a real problem.

The good news is that there is an antidote to this type of thinking. It is the middle way. By taking a little time and space for ourselves so we can identify and deal with any emptiness or frustrations we feel, we begin to fill ourselves up—and instead of our self-focus *taking away* from the family, our increased sense of well-being *gives so much more* to it. When we feel more complete, it is easier to give to others.

Feelings of low self-worth can lead to over-functioning.
Over-functioning is also a way to compensate for feelings of low self-worth or self-esteem. Unfortunately, striving to be a perfect mother, wife, housewife, etc., doesn't work to raise your self-worth. Self-worth is actually an inner job. It stems from a deep sense that your mere existence matters and is not dependent on your external achievements. External achievements cannot erase low self-worth.

When the things outside ourselves are too important, we end up minimizing what's inside. We are no longer in touch with our own feelings. We often don't know what we need. We draw a blank when we are asked what we want. We don't spend time nurturing our dreams and desires. Heck, who has time for those? Yet, we seem to know what everyone else needs and wants. We know what *they* dream of. We have difficulty spending time, energy, and money on our own personal growth and needs, but we run around trying to make sure others are fulfilled. When our children grow up and don't need us as much, we often don't know what to do with ourselves.

When your "doings" are not making you feel better, you might find yourself becoming impatient, moody, stressed, fatigued, or even depressed. You end up snapping at your kids and husbands and then feel guilty about it. Contentment eludes you. Resentment creeps in.

Can you relate? Human *doings* substitute activity for living. Making sure everything is done, and done "perfectly," keeps moms distracted from any unrest, dissatisfaction, or emptiness that might be brewing. *Doing* replaces *being* and the family just ticks right along. Except when you can't do all the doing and then you feel bad and guilty. It's a vicious cycle. It's the proverbial squirrel cage.

Ironically, when over-functioning people do find time for themselves, they often overbook themselves with activities, obligations, classes, or other pursuits that push them into *more* doing. Precious "me time" turns into more over-functioning when you are not able to identify what it is you really want and need. You lose yourself in an activity that is not connected to your deeper values and dreams. I'm exhausted just thinking about it!

Over-functioning can lead to "over-parenting."
There is no question that mothering is a demanding role and job. It does not, however, mean losing yourself. Recently, research has emerged to address what some experts are calling "over-parenting" or "hyper-parenting." Studies show that out of anxiety or ambition, parents hover so closely over their children that they overdo what are seemingly good intentions to ensure a great future for them.

Mothers can take on this management role of their children's lives. Unfortunately, in the process of managing their children's lives, mothers are not fostering independence in their children and lose sight of their own lives. Author Hara Estroff Marano writes that the risk of "over-parenting" is greater for mothers who have left the work force to stay at home full-time. Because they have sacrificed their own jobs and ambitions in order to do what they think is best for their children, they really want that sacrifice to be worth it. So, they pour their heart and soul into their children's lives.

We cannot feel complete by living someone else's life. We have to strive to fulfill some of our own desires as well. Many of my over-functioning clients began that journey by attending a monthly coaching group or did individual coaching that was focused on them, *not* on parenting and *not* on their children. Rather than rocking the boat as they had initially feared, they gained more balance in their lives. Some of them managed to give over age appropriate responsibilities to their children. And, for all of them, family life improved.

3. Guilt

Did I just hear a collective groan? I know. Guilt is such a huge topic that I could write a whole book about it. But what a depressing book that would be! It is a huge topic because it is one of the prevailing emotions all mothers feel, and feel a lot. These feelings of guilt are another very painful way that mothers lose themselves.

Every mother I've ever worked with has suffered from

guilt at some point. I hear stories about how they can feel guilty when they are coming and when they are going. They feel guilty when they don't do enough, and they can *never* do enough, because their tasks never end. They feel guilty when their own needs interfere with the needs of others.

Some mothers talk about feeling guilty when they spend time on themselves because they think they are neglecting others and letting them down. Then they feel guilty when they spend so much time on others that they neglect themselves. Some mothers feel guilty because they are often so lovingly attached to their babies they let other things slide, like their health or appearance or their relationships with friends, family members, and spouses.

One client told me that she often feels guilty after dinner when she is cleaning up the kitchen instead of reading to her children. But then, when she leaves the mess for later, she feels guilty about that, too! It's a no-win situation.

Guilt does have its place. Healthy guilt happens when you actually do something wrong, like steal, cheat, lie, etc. It can be a helpful inner voice of conscience that makes all of us productive members of a civil society.

That is not the guilt I am talking about here. It feels similar to healthy guilt in that a mother *feels* she is doing something wrong. But in this case, it is a false idea of "wrong." What she is doing "wrong," in her mind, is not living up to unrealistically high standards and expectations of what it means to be a good mother.

Mothers feel guilt when they don't live up to society's standards for being a good mother.

It might be an image she holds of the perfect homemaker like Martha Stewart that haunts her. It might be the onslaught of cheerful mothers and housewives that flash before us every day in TV commercials. It might be the perfect 1950s mother and housewife like June Cleaver from the television show *Leave It to Beaver*. It might even be an idealized image of her own mother or grandmother, or even her idea of the other mothers she sees at the park, at soccer practice, or at school. Her high expectations of herself may also be a reaction to what she saw as lacking in her own mother.

Feelings of guilt are produced whenever you feel bad for not being able to live up to those images of the ideal mother and wife, when you fall short of being perfect and you think you have let people down. The problem is, all those ideals aren't real. They are totally and completely made up. They are phoney-baloney, fantasies, not even close to the truth. False. False. False.

Can I stress this enough? The expectation that you as a mother should be able to live up to those ideals is totally and painfully unrealistic. So you end up feeling guilty for not living up to something that is actually impossible to live up to, because it isn't real. Not real. Not possible to live up to. Airbrushed. Created by someone out of his or her own fantasies. Fiction.

Hopefully, I have made my point.

I see mothers being terribly hard on themselves. They become so critical of themselves each time they don't meet these impossible standards. I often ask them in coaching if they would talk to their friends in the judgmental, non-compassionate way that they talk to themselves when they fall short of the ideal.

Of course I wouldn't, they say.

Then why, I ask them, *is it okay to treat yourself that way?*

You have a right to be happy.
This is where the second underlying cause of guilt creeps in. Somewhere deep within, so many mothers don't believe they have a right to be happy. They believe that everyone else's happiness is more important than their own. Nathaniel Branden, a leading expert in self-esteem, sees a person's confidence in their right to be happy as the basis for self-worth, one of the two cornerstones of healthy self-esteem. The other is self-efficacy, the feeling that one is up to the challenges of life.

Once a woman recognizes her own intrinsic value as a whole person and not just in the role of wife or mother, she will feel less guilty about reconnecting with herself, focusing on her own fulfillment, and becoming more complete. To do that, she must believe that she has a right to be happy, too. Happiness is not just for other people.

So, are you feeling guilty about feeling guilty yet? It is good practice to check and see if your feelings of guilt are truly coming from you doing something that goes against your values and morals. If they are, let your guilt guide you to making amends. If your feelings of guilt are coming from having unrealistic expectations of yourself that you can't live up to and feeling you are letting yourself and others down, then do your best to find compassion for yourself and remind yourself that "useless guilt" only serves to make you unhappy and keep you down. You do not deserve it. You have a right to be happy.

4. People-pleasing

The process of losing yourself is a subtle one. I have some clients who can trace it back to before they had children, to much earlier in their relationships with their husbands or partners. Women tell me they remember moments when they felt swept up in the romance of their lives and allowed things that they didn't totally agree with to be "okay." Some women are conditioned to believe that it is their role to accommodate more than their spouses.

I had one client tell me that she didn't really take enough time to think about what it would mean to her in the long run to stay at home full-time with her children. She knew what she would be gaining, but she didn't face up to what she was losing. She also knew it was very important to her husband that she be at home for the kids, which made it important to her.

Mothers suffer from the "disease to please."

Many women in my practice suffer from what Oprah Winfrey calls "the disease to please." A woman's need to please others can cause her to lose touch with her own needs and wants. When she becomes a mother, she wants to make sure her children are happy, so whether it's from exhaustion, frustration, or a desire for temporary peace, she gives in to please them.

People-pleasing is very sneaky. So many times, we don't even realize we are doing it. It might start with little things that don't really mean much, like choosing a restaurant or a movie to go to. When we are people-pleasing we tend to go along with what others want rather than making our desires known.

Over time, these little moments of people-pleasing can really add up. One mother told me that during the coaching process she sort of "woke up" and realized that because of all the little ways she was constantly accommodating and people-pleasing, she had become a different person. She wondered what had happened to the young woman she used to be. She remembered how she had energy and passion for her life and dreams. She remembered how she knew what she wanted and wasn't afraid to ask for it. Sadly, because of her need to please others, she had sublimated her own desires in so many small ways, and lost herself.

People-pleasing leads to resentment.
Losing oneself in people-pleasing means we tend to say yes when we really mean no and vice versa. Sometimes we don't speak up when we disagree or have our own ideas about things. We feel that these little things are not worth the trouble. It is easy to see how resentment can creep in here.

At a certain point, we begin to feel undervalued and taken advantage of. It can be very difficult to face the ways we have contributed to this state ourselves.

However, facing up to the ways we have abandoned ourselves in our relationships is imperative for a fulfilled and complete life. Your complete self exists within you, no matter how much people-pleasing you may have done. It is in you and you can find it.

THE BENEFITS OF FULFILLING THE LONGING OF YOUR SOUL

Letting go of self-sacrifice, over-functioning, unhealthy guilt, and people-pleasing frees both you and your children. Learning to balance your life will reduce stress, facilitate relationships, and allow you to be more truly present in all aspects of your life. You will begin to experience more and more moments of joy.

A more complete you gives your children the permission to go out and live their lives to the fullest. You stop any legacy of guilt being passed down. In addition, your children learn about confidence, self-esteem, and self-reliance from your example. As a result, they emerge less self-centered and able to have empathy.

Finally, focusing some attention on the longing of your soul will help you to feel so much more alive and energized overall. Reconnecting with your needs and then asking for them to be addressed is very empowering.

There is no doubt that the process of fulfilling yourself is challenging. It is tough to look at yourself this deeply. It hurts and it can sometimes feel overwhelming, but following the coaching process in Part Two of this book will make it easier. In addition, the Mothers on Fire weekly ezine features valuable tips and personal experiences to help you through this process. You can subscribe to this ezine by going to www.mothersonfire.com. It helps to keep the end goal in mind by focusing on the wonderful benefits that feeling complete has in store for you and your family. Remind yourself of the benefits often while you are working through the coaching program, especially at times when you might feel doubtful and discouraged.

CHAPTER ONE: SUMMARY

+ In any relationship based on love, it is extremely important to maintain your sense of self.

+ Loving others does not mean you have to lose yourself.

+ A mother's sense of self-worth and self-esteem can become attached to how well she perceives herself to be performing in her job as a mother and how well her children perform.

+ If she is not careful, a mother can become less involved in her own life and over-involved in her children's lives.

✦ There are four ways mothers lose themselves:
  - Self-sacrifice
  - Over-functioning
  - Guilt
  - People-pleasing

✦ Letting go of self-sacrifice, over-functioning, unhealthy guilt, and people-pleasing frees both you and your children.

✦ A more complete you gives your children the permission to go out and live their lives to the fullest.

WHAT IS A
MOTHER ON FIRE?

*For it's not light that is needed, but fire;
it's not the gentle shower, but thunder.
We need the storm, the whirlwind
and the earthquake in our hearts.*

—Frederick Douglass, American abolitionist,
women's suffragist, editor, orator,
author, statesman, and reformer

If the problem for North American mothers is that they lose sight of who they are, then a Mother on Fire is a woman who knows who she is and is more fully herself. Even though the seemingly all-consuming nature of motherhood might cause her children and even her spouse to see her only as "mommy," a complete mother works hard at staying connected to the many different dimensions of herself.

Instead of being lost in her role, a mother who knows herself recognizes she is a unique individual. She is connected to her needs, wants, dreams, longings, and preferences. She is also kinder to herself. When a mother has found herself again, she is able to be more accepting and forgiving of her many traits and behaviors. She is able to share her dreams, even if they seem out of sync with her role as a mother.

At a deep level, connecting to her many dimensions means that a mother learns to pay attention to and live out of the longing of her soul. It means allowing meaning and purpose and self-fulfillment into her life even if some of that lies beyond her role as a mother. It means she feels energized and passionate about life. It means she is on fire.

THE TEN CHARACTERISTICS OF A MOTHER ON FIRE

1. A Mother on Fire believes she has a right to be happy.
Believing that one has a right to be happy is fundamental to one's self-esteem. Without this fundamental belief, a mother will focus on everyone else's happiness and either forget about or ignore her own, and ultimately start to resent it. Often, mothers don't even realize they have this negative mindset. When they do accept that they have a right to be happy too, they learn to stop sacrificing their own needs.

2. A Mother on Fire starts from where she is.
A Mother on Fire gives up the excuses she has for why she can't make changes or shouldn't fulfill herself. Instead, she faces the reality of her life as it is today and accepts it. She realizes that *now* is the time. Tomorrow hasn't happened yet and yesterday is gone. Wherever she is today, whether it's

kids in diapers, kids in college, kids all over the place, NOW is her point of power. This time and place is the right and only time and place to start paying attention to the longing of her soul and the broadening of her life.

3. A Mother on Fire is awake, conscious, and self-aware.

Many mothers—and people in general—go through their lives without a lot of self-awareness. Yet, raising one's self-awareness leads to a stronger sense of well-being and freedom. For example, the practice of psychoanalysis claims that people can be relieved of certain neuroses by making their unconscious conscious. Even the Eastern traditions like Hinduism and Yoga suggest that we live our lives in an almost dream state and that raising our state of consciousness is really waking up. Transfer this idea of waking up to a mother's life and what you have is a lot more enjoyment. Mothers who are awake are more aware of what they are feeling and what they need and want. This is crucial to living from the longing of your soul. When you stay asleep, life just passes you by.

4. A Mother on Fire realizes and accepts that she creates her life.

Oh, how easy it is to blame others for our misery—or to credit others for our joy. True happiness comes from the knowledge and complete acceptance that we create our own lives. Things do happen to us, but it is our interpretation of and response to those things that determine our reaction. You cannot be happy or fulfilled if you see yourself as a victim. Taking healthy responsibility for your life, your feelings, and your choices, lifts you out of the dark pit of victimhood and into the sunlight of personal fulfillment and growth. Doesn't that sound a lot better?

5. *A Mother on Fire is a human being.*

I talked earlier about how mothers become human *doings*, or doing machines, functioning and over-functioning endlessly. A Mother on Fire not only slows down a little, she also goes within. She finds ways to connect with her inner life, with her inner being, and that inner fire that might have been lying dormant. By developing and nurturing the relationship with one's inner self, one's outer self blossoms. *Being* replaces *doing* and life takes on a very different hue and tone. Daily activities become more fulfilling. You create powerful and real relationships with people, including your kids and husband. You become a real person and not just a wind-up toy.

6. *A Mother on Fire knows she is more than "just a mom."*

Becoming a parent can really trigger an identity crisis. It feels so natural to give oneself over to it whole-heartedly. It feels as if we must do that to protect our children and to be seen as a good mother. A Mother on Fire is a dedicated mother to be sure, but she also allows herself to stay connected to the many other aspects of herself.

7. *A Mother on Fire has focus, vision, and dreams for herself.*

At the beginning of a coaching session, I often ask clients to share their dreams. Most mothers have trouble with this.

They often say that they know their children's dreams and they know their husbands' dreams, but they don't have a clue about their own. After a little coaching, they get a lot clearer about what they want for themselves. The dream may start small at first, but after a while I have seen some mothers reconnect to some pretty large and powerful dreams that had been hidden within. Whatever the size of the dream, what matters is that it is *your own* dream.

8. A Mother on Fire takes time to nurture herself.

Most books for mothers are about parenting and nurturing children. But what about nurturing mothers? Doesn't it make sense that the healthier and happier the mother, the better care she can give to her children? Every flight attendant and airline safety manual points out that you need to put your own oxygen mask on before you can assist others. That is a valuable analogy for a mother. Your self-care becomes a priority so that you can be at your best for others. As one mother said to me, *After I spent that hour working on my dream, I had so much more to give to my daughter.*

9. A Mother on Fire allows herself to be herself.

Many mothers hide their true thoughts and feelings because they feel ashamed. One mother told me that for a long time she felt too ashamed or self-conscious to talk with other people about how angry she could get at her daughter sometimes. But when she accepted that she was by nature an intense person who occasionally had intense reactions, she began to be more open about the issue with other mothers.

Sure enough, she began to see that lots of other mothers had struggled or were struggling with the same thing. Once she understood that, she felt liberated.

10. A Mother on Fire realizes that she doesn't have to be perfect to be a good enough mother.

Somehow, maybe in early childhood, many of us were conditioned to believe we had to be perfect to be good enough. Perfectionism, however, is an obsession and does not support our well-being. A mother must learn to let go of the obsession with perfection if she wants to find herself again. Life is messy, everybody makes mistakes, things happen that we cannot control, and that is all okay.

Are you a Mother on Fire?
Go to www.mothersonfire.com
and download a questionnaire to
determine if you are on fire.

WE ALL ONLY GET ONE LIFE

When a mother loses herself, it is as if she is giving her life up and living someone else's life. That means your one life goes by without your full participation.

Many mothers I know whose children are grown and living on their own look back on their childrearing years and wonder why they lost themselves. Some feel a little regret when they realize they got too focused on their roles and forgot how to be "real."

You don't have to do that. Becoming a Mother on Fire will save you from that regret. By connecting to all the dimensions of yourself again, you get your life back and so much more because in the act of reconnecting with yourself, you will discover that there is more within you than you realized. Your one life becomes a very full and complete life. You learn to satisfy the longing of your soul and you get to live like a Mother on Fire.

CHAPTER TWO: SUMMARY

✦ A Mother on Fire feels more complete. She is a woman who knows who she is and is more fully herself. She works hard at staying connected to the many different dimensions of herself.

✦ There are ten characteristics of a Mother on Fire:

1. She believes she has a right to be happy. This is fundamental to one's self-esteem.

2. She starts from where she is instead of waiting for just the right time. She faces the reality of her life as it is today and accepts it. Now is the time.

3. She is awake, conscious, and self-aware. Raising one's self-awareness leads to a stronger sense of well-being and freedom.

4. She realizes and accepts that she creates her life. You cannot be happy or fulfilled if you see yourself as a victim.

5. She is a human *being* rather than a human *doing*. You find ways to connect with your inner being and your inner fire that might have been lying dormant.

6. She knows that she is more than "just a mom." She is a dedicated mother, but she also allows herself to be more fully and completely herself.

7. She has focus, vision, and dreams for herself.

8. She takes time to nurture herself. The healthier and happier the mother, the better care she can give to her children.

9. She allows herself to be herself.

10. She realizes that she doesn't have to be perfect to be a good enough mother. A mother must learn to let go of the obsession with perfection if she wants to find herself again.

◆ When a mother loses herself, it is as if she is giving her life up and living someone else's life. Your life goes by without your full participation.

◆ By connecting to all dimensions of yourself, you get your life back. Your life becomes a very full and complete life and you get to live like a Mother on Fire.

Visit www.mothersonfire.com and read "Meet a Mother on Fire" to learn how moms like you became Mothers on Fire.

3

OVERCOMING OBSTACLES TO CHANGE

Motivation is a fire from within. If someone else tries to light that fire under you, chances are it will burn very briefly.

—Stephen Covey, author

When is it the right time to reconnect with your lost self, feel more complete, connect with your soul's longing, and work on the Mothers on Fire Coaching Program™?

I'll get back to you on that, Lisa, as soon as the kids are in school full-time.

Is it after the dishes are done and the laundry is put away? Is it once the kids are out of diapers? What about when your husband isn't working such long hours or when you have saved more money?

College, I think. Yes, when the children are in college. That is the perfect time.

Many of the mothers in my coaching groups and one-on-one sessions talk about getting their lives in perfect order, waiting for obstacles to clear or milestones to be reached—

or just for a better time—before they can start to focus a little on their own fulfillment.

The perceived need to get our lives in perfect order is a form of resistance and points to a few underlying obstacles mothers in particular experience when they are contemplating change.

OBSTACLES TO CHANGE

Change is scary.
First, there is fear. Change makes people anxious. It is common for people to have a fear of the unknown. We worry that it might not be for the better or that we might not be able to cope with something new and different. For mothers whose instincts are so profoundly focused on preservation and protection, change can feel threatening. For you to make changes towards feeling more complete, you are going to need to muster up your courage.

Change is hard work.
Change is also difficult because it requires effort. We all get into habits of thoughts and behaviors that feel easy. We may not want them anymore, but changing them feels hard to do. It is always so much easier to slide down the hill than to climb back up. That is what change feels like: it feels like climbing up a great big hill. Ugh! Trying to muster the energy and momentum to get up that big hill of change is especially tough for mothers who are often overtired and stressed to begin with.

Sometimes we are just stuck.

Finally, sometimes, no matter how much we want to change something, we feel we just can't. We are simply "stuck." So many mothers feel this way. They know they need to change things—maybe eat better, get out to see friends more, or not get so angry at the kids—but they are so overwhelmed, they just can't do it. It feels like a big weight on top of them.

One mother told me that even though she knew what to do to change things, she just couldn't get her feet off the ground. She couldn't find the drive. She believed that in her first year as a mother, she was stuck because she was depressed. Along with the physiological and chemical changes of pregnancy and birth, she had the psychological and mental challenges of dealing with just how much parenthood had changed her life. She said it was like a grieving process where she was dealing with the feelings of loss around her former life and her relationships beyond her baby.

Living out of the longing of your soul is risky.

Becoming a mother is not all sunshine and roses, is it. Much like the reality of marriage after the honeymoon, the reality of motherhood can be disillusioning at times. It is a lot to face up to. It feels risky to face your underlying fears and blocks, deal with self-recriminations for "not getting it together," and admit to the worry that you might not be up to the task of managing your life well.

Like a real fire, feeling more complete through the work you will do in the Mothers on Fire Coaching Program™ can be hard to handle at times. But, people can be trained to conduct what forestry and agricultural experts call "controlled burns." You can, too. You can weed out what is unwanted and plant anew. Getting past these obstacles and into the life you crave is possible.

DEALING WITH CHANGE

Change requires a shift in thinking.
Whatever the obstacle you are experiencing, you will need a shift in your thinking to help you over, around, under, or through it. If you are feeling anxious about facing yourself and your life head on, you will need to shift out of thoughts of fear and into thoughts that calm you down.

If your confidence is low, you will need to shift into thoughts that will be less critical and more supportive.

And, if you are stuck, you will need to develop thoughts that will help you to move those feet forward.

Your frame of mind and your habitual thoughts impact your potential to make changes and feel complete more than you might realize. Thought always precedes action, so when your thoughts are moving you forward, your actions will follow. And, with enough consistent, positive actions, lives change.

But, before you can work on your thinking, you have to know *what* you are thinking. Creating a journaling habit is a great way to recognize your thought patterns.

Journaling is a great tool to help you overcome your obstacles to change.

Writing is a powerful tool for change. Before you get too worried about it, no one other than you needs to read it unless you ask them to. No one will be marking it. Journaling is your way of developing a stronger, more empowering relationship with yourself. It will allow you to keep track of how you are feeling. It helps you to sort out problems that seem all jumbled up when you keep them in your head. In addition, journaling will give you a record of how far you have come on your journey of self-discovery.

A journal is one place you can discover your lost self and reconnect with your soul's longing. Because journaling is just for you and no one else, you can set up the rules any way you like. You might take five minutes before bed to jot down your thoughts about your day. You might find fifteen minutes on a Sunday afternoon with a cup of coffee or tea to review your week. If you have older children, you could set up a quiet time each evening when everybody sits down and journals as a family. Or, you can write while the children read, do homework, or draw.

I encourage you to make a journaling date with yourself at least once each week as your first commitment to your own fulfillment. Believe me, you will have lots to write about as you work through the exercises in this book.

Studies show that the quality of one's thinking predicts the level of success one achieves in life. Journaling will help you to develop more successful thought patterns, ones that will support you in your quest for positive change.

Journaling through fear, lack of confidence, and inertia.
Along with discovering things about yourself, journaling can help you to uncover the layers of resistance that prevent you from fulfilling the longing of your soul and making changes. In time, you will come to recognize the thought patterns that serve and support you versus the ones that keep you down. Before too long, you will be able to switch out of the detrimental patterns and into the ones that will propel you to greater fulfillment.

Those unsupportive thought patterns are downright critical. That is why many people in the personal development field call those critical thoughts the voice of your inner critic.

We all have an inner voice that sometimes says things that hold us back. This voice is natural and normal. The purpose of that voice is to keep us in a state of homeostasis—the tendency to maintain the status quo. You can expect that when you start to contemplate moving forward, making changes or going after a big dream, that inner voice will chime in with lots of thoughts that are critical and not helpful.

> The Mothers on Fire weekly ezine often includes queries and questions that will provide prompts to help you with your journaling. You can subscribe to this ezine by going to www.mothersonfire.com.

The bigger the change or dream, the stronger the resistance.

Perhaps you've heard this inner voice referred to as negative self-talk. Author Richard Carson calls it "The Gremlin." He describes it as the metaphorical embodiment of thoughts and feelings that seem to have only one purpose—to make us miserable.

That inner critic can be *very* critical. Not only can it prevent you from taking action by creating worse case scenarios and doubts in your head, but it can reprimand you for *not* taking action, too!

A losing battle, to be sure. Carson writes that it is helpful if we don't judge the Gremlin voice, but accept that it just is and allow it to be. That is because if we spend too much time fighting with it, it catches us in its clever web of negativity and lo and behold, we get stuck like glue.

Our negative self-talk can sound so reasonable even when it's not.

Negative self-talk is tricky and sticky and even a little slippery because sometimes it sounds so reasonable and right. For example, I have one client who has some fantastic ideas for a series of fun games moms can play with their children to help them understand elementary math. She is just full of passion when she talks about it. She has great ideas on what her product would look like and even how to market it. When she shared this with her coaching group, they were all astounded and excited for her. She had been searching for something to inspire her aside from being a mom and there it was, clear as day.

And then, negativity descended like the proverbial dark cloud. We all saw the light drain from her eyes as she rhymed off all the reasons why she could not and would not do any of it. That was her Gremlin talking. And yet, it all sounded so reasonable.

Our negative voices may indeed be reasonable and even right about some things. But, it is only one perspective. There are always several perspectives in every situation. The Gremlin will try to convince you that its voice is the right and holy one. But it's not. It's just the negative one.

Journaling helps you to manage the critical voice.
As a coach, I can hear the critical inner voice of a client pretty clearly. But it is much harder to hear it in ourselves because we are so used to it. Journaling can help you to isolate that voice so you can learn to manage it better. You will notice in time that when you are connected to yourself through your dreams and passions and the longing of your soul, you have energy. You feel alive. Your thoughts may reflect the challenges, but that is all they are, challenges to work through.

In contrast, when the critical voice is in charge, you feel drained. You often experience mental fog or get caught in a tangle of arguments. The problems weigh you down and feel bigger than you. Your thinking keeps going around and around in circles over the same issues without seeing other options. Coaches call this "circling Dallas."

There are several journaling exercises in Part Two of this book. The more you journal, the more you will notice how your negative thoughts or positive focus affect your moods. Turn to your positive focus as much as possible every day. See if you can talk to people from that perspective more often. What you will notice is that you are complaining less and feeling good about your life more. It is hard work, though. It takes effort because the negative perspective always feels easier somehow. Perhaps it seems easier because it has become a habit. Putting the effort into changing the negative habit is worth it. The energy of your positive focus will help to motivate and inspire you from within as you start working through the Mothers on Fire Coaching Program™ in Part Two of this book.

CHAPTER THREE: SUMMARY

+ Many mothers believe the time needs to be *perfect* before they can start to focus on their own fulfillment.

+ Even though their reasons for not changing seem so real and legitimate, the underlying reason is usually some form of fear that is holding them back from making changes.

+ Change requires a shift in thinking. You will need to shift out of thoughts of fear and into less critical and more supportive thoughts.

+ The inner critic is the voice in your head that thinks it is keeping you safe when in fact it is just keeping you down.

✦ Journaling will help you to develop a more empowering relationship with yourself. It will help you to isolate that negative voice so you can learn to manage it better. Make a journaling date with yourself at least once each week.

✦ When the critical voice is in charge, you feel drained. When you connect to your dreams, passions, and the longing of your soul, you have energy.

✦ Remember to turn to your positive focus as much as possible every day. You will find yourself complaining less and feeling better about your life more.

PART TWO

THE MOTHERS ON FIRE COACHING PROGRAM™

GETTING STARTED

Success is not the result of spontaneous combustion. You must first set yourself on fire.

—Fred Shero, coach of Stanley Cup–winning hockey team

STEP ONE:
DECIDE TO BUILD YOUR INNER FIRE

It's time to get started on finding your authentic self, being more complete, and becoming a Mother on Fire. The longing of your soul is waiting to be fulfilled. Hopefully, you are chomping at the bit to get going. Right?

Well, not quite, Lisa. I am a little overwhelmed at the moment.

Understandable. The path to fulfillment is not always a yellow brick road. If it were, you'd be on it by now. So let's break it down into some steps for you to follow. Let's use our fire metaphor as a guide. How do you build a fire? You don't start with the huge logs that are too heavy to lift. You can't just flick a spark under big branches and expect a roaring flame.

To build a roaring fire, we start with the small stuff and work up to the big stuff. The same is true when you are building your inner fire. There are several steps you must go through. First, you have to decide to build it. Second, you need to survey the land. Third, you are ready to spark your fire. Once you have the spark, you can lay on the kindling and small branches to get it going. Finally, you can add the really big logs. Okay?

Okay. Yes. I feel better now.

Great. Let's go.

Every action starts with a decision.

When you are out camping or sitting in your living room, you get a fire started by first deciding to light one. Isn't that true? Well, lighting your inner fire and working on your fulfillment starts with a decision too, but not just any old decision. It must be a conscious and determined decision for it to have any power. Every action, like getting a new job or just figuring out what to eat for dinner is preceded by a decision. If you want to know how you got to where you are today, take a look at the decisions you made or failed to make over your lifetime.

Something as deep and as meaningful as personal fulfillment demands that you make a commitment. It must become a priority; otherwise, life has a way of interfering and taking you off track.

Your decision has power.

Your personal decision acts like an anchor for you on your journey. It will help you to build the burning desire necessary to stay the course when life tries to seduce you into giving up and taking a different road.

A conscious decision has power. Faith, commitment, purpose, intention, and determination are all parts of a powerful decision. You are making a conscious and committed choice for something you really want. You are saying "no" to choices that could take you off track. Every decision moves you either closer to or farther from what you want.

Deciding has more purpose than a wish and more power than a longing. For example, when I went to university at the age of thirty-three, I was a high school dropout. Yes, I ran away from home at sixteen to join the circus—well, not exactly a circus, but close. I joined a rock band.

At thirty-three, I decided to change my life again, so I thought I'd go to university and discover myself. But, there were people in my life who were a little concerned.

A high school dropout at university? Does she know what she's getting into?

What they didn't know was that I had made a decision. It was a very committed decision to do whatever it took for me to succeed. Period. That decision got me through a lot of very hard times and huge challenges. It kept me going because I did whatever it took. In the end, I had the most exciting years of my life, culminating with a graduate degree in psychology. But, without that decision, that powerful commitment, I don't think I could have done it.

Exercise: Reflect on the Decisions in Your Life

1. Think of a time when you simply wished or hoped for something. What was that like for you? How did you feel? For example, one mom remembered what it was like to wish she could leave her rental house and buy her own home:

> *Things that were not ideal about our living conditions started to irk me more and more as the prospect of buying property drifted further and further away. I spent a year and a half feeling discouraged and wishful. I wished that we could own a house, even hoped for some kind of windfall to make it possible, but neither of those things were realistically going to happen. In other words, my attitude stank. Being wishful just made me feel even more dissatisfied, and stuck.*

2. Now think about how you felt when you made a decision about something. How did your decision help you? Could you feel your determination to see it through? Here's what happened for the mom above when she made a decision to make the most of her situation:

> *It was crazy to suddenly start feeling like our lack of material wealth indicated a lack of success. So my husband and I talked about what we could do to improve our living conditions and bring a personal touch into our home. We got the neighbor to scrap the broken-down eyesore of a car that was blocking the*

driveway and our path to the backyard. We painted the walls of the main floor and part of the upstairs in colors that better reflected our style. We hung shelves for better organization. We asked the landlord to do some much-needed repairs. We sifted through all the belongings we had stored in giant, disorganized heaps in the basement and set aside items for a yard sale. We spoke to the owner of the house next door about our noise issues with the tenants. And the list goes on . . .

My whole outlook changed. Suddenly I didn't feel held back by our situation. I am comfortable here, and am able to face the reality of having to wait to buy a house. When something in the house starts to bother me, I do something about it.

Can't you just feel the motivational power she got when she made a decision to change her situation rather than just wish it were different? That is why we start this process of change with a decision.

Exercise: Make a Decision

As I mentioned earlier, the life coaching process in this book is not a quick-fix scheme. It takes work and guts to seek your own happiness and fulfillment in the midst of the chaos and demands of motherhood. You need to be as committed to yourself as you are to your family. If you are not, you just won't do it. You really need to make a decision to propel you into action. And, you need to remind yourself of your decision regularly.

1. Ask yourself: "What decision can I make right now that will support my commitment to finding myself, feeling complete, and becoming a Mother on Fire?"

2. Write out your decision in your journal.

3. Do a gut check. Can you feel your decision in your gut? Do you get a little flutter of excitement within? If not, try some other decisions until you feel you've got one that resonates with you. Then rewrite it somewhere where you can read it often to remind yourself of your decision.

Here are some ideas if you are feeling stuck and unable to come up with a powerful decision:

+ I intend to find myself again.
+ I will nurture my whole being.
+ I am determined to find more joy in my life.
+ I WILL follow my bliss.
+ I've decided to pay more attention to my own needs.
+ I've decided to become a Mother on Fire.

EXERCISE: FIND AN INSPIRATIONAL SONG

I love music. Some songs just make me get up and dance and some make me sit down and cry. How about you? Think of a song that inspires you, makes you feel really alive, and reminds you of your decision. Better yet, pick more than one, for different moods. But, make sure you *really* love the song, because hopefully you're going to play it a lot.

Here are some favorites from the Mothers on Fire workshops to get you started:

- Amy Sky: "Phenomenal Woman"

- Bruce Springsteen: "Born to Run"

- Diana Ross: "I'm Coming Out"

- Natasha Bedingfield: "Unwritten"

- Jill Scott: "Golden"

- Coldplay: "Fix You"

- Macy Gray: "A Moment to Myself"

- Bachman-Turner Overdrive: "Taking Care of Business"

Play your song(s) whenever you need a boost of energy. Download your inspirational song or songs on your MP3 player and listen to it when completing your everyday tasks, like laundry and dishes. Life just feels better when you are rocking to your favorite tunes. I like playing sexy jazz when I am cleaning the house. It makes me feel like I am in a French film! Let the vibrations of the music lift you up and broadcast to the universe that you are here in all your glory. I can hear it now. "I'm coming out." La la la la!

Check out the playlist recommendations on the Mothers on Fire website for more of our favorite songs. Some are inspirational, while others are just plain fun. www.mothersonfire.com

Decisions wake up your inner critic.

Making a decision to commit time, energy, and focus on yourself is Step One in the Mothers on Fire Coaching Program™. It is a short step, but it is a powerful one. In fact, because it is so powerful, it will likely awaken your inner critic. You can get past some of your inner critic's objections by learning to switch out of its negative focus and into the compelling reasons why you want to become a Mother on Fire. This exercise will teach you how to connect with a more positive perspective, something you will need to do often as you build your inner fire.

EXERCISE: SWITCHING FROM NEGATIVE FOCUS TO POSITIVE FOCUS

1   Take a sheet of paper and draw a vertical line down the center. Title the left-hand column *Negative Focus* and right-hand column *Positive Focus*. Now write down the objections, doubts, or beliefs that are negative and limiting. They are the thoughts that are telling you that becoming a Mother on Fire is stupid or silly or impossible. Just let it flow. It is amazing how much relief you can feel by getting the negativity out of your head and onto paper. (See example on page 63.)

2. Now let your positive focus have a say. Connect with the excitement and the energy of becoming a Mother on Fire. Let yourself talk about why you want to do it. Make the reasons as compelling as possible. Dream about how you

NEGATIVE FOCUS	POSITIVE FOCUS
So, I am a stay-at-home mom and I don't know who I am anymore. I've decided to find myself. Big deal. How much time can I possibly give to this? I am in over my head already.	Why do I want to become a Mother on Fire?
I figure this is what it means to stay at home. I don't get to have a life.	I get a little excited just thinking about what that is. I want to make sure that staying at home is going to be a good experience for me.
Everyone is dependent on me and if I change things I could cause a real upheaval that would make people unhappy.	I want to enjoy my life and my children and make sure my relationship is strong.
What will people say if I tell them I am working on becoming a Mother on Fire? They'll probably laugh. I am not sure I even understand why I am doing this. I am not even sure I know what it is!	There is a lot inside of me that wants to come out. I mean, I have been pretty accomplished in my life so far and I want to continue that.
Who am I kidding?	I am still young. I have so much life to live. I really want to live it. I want to be on fire.
	I bet being a Mother on Fire will be a great thing for my kids, too. I want to be a good role model for them.
	And, I want to stay interesting to my husband.

want to be and how you want to feel. If another negative thought pops up, write it down on the left side, in the *Negative Focus* column.

3. Review the energy and excitement in the Positive Focus column often.

Connecting with the positive and compelling reasons for

becoming a Mother on Fire is a big part of life coaching. It isn't about getting rid of all the negative stuff that is keeping you down, it's about helping you to focus your attention more on the good stuff. It's about changing the balance so that you are connected more to what you want for your life rather than what you don't want. It shifts you out of why you can't have it to why you want it in the first place. This exercise helps you to connect more and more with the passion and excitement that lives inside you now. Learning to shift into a positive focus helps you to become a Mother on Fire.

Making a decision is the step that gets you up and moving in the direction of your personal fulfillment. Once you are clear and excited about your decision, you are ready to move on to Step Two: Surveying the Territory.

CHAPTER FOUR: SUMMARY

+ When you start to build your inner fire, it is important to take it one step at a time so you don't get overwhelmed.

+ Finding your authentic self starts with a conscious and determined decision.

+ Something as deep and meaningful as lighting your inner fire and working on your fulfillment demands that you make a commitment. It must become a priority; otherwise, life has a way of interfering and taking you off track.

+ A conscious decision has power. Deciding has more purpose than a wish and more power than a longing.

✦ Find a song that really inspires you and play it often to remind you of your decision.

✦ Learning to switch from a negative focus to a positive focus can help you to get past some of your inner critic's objections.

✦ Having a positive focus will help you to connect with your passion and excitement.

5

TAKING STOCK
OF YOUR LIFE

*Life is either a daring adventure
or nothing.*

—Helen Keller, author, political
activist, and lecturer

STEP TWO:
SURVEYING THE TERRITORY

In Step One, you made a decision to light your inner fire, feel more complete, and strive to become a Mother on Fire. With an actual fire, you would survey the area to see what material was there to use for it. Are there large logs around? What about smaller branches? Will the sparks or smoke cause a problem for anyone? Are there any safety issues?

Building your inner fire is similar. You will need to survey where you are standing in your life right now and take stock. A coaching tool called the Wheel of Life is great for this survey. It helps people get a general idea of "where" they are starting from and what they have to work with. It will help you to get oriented as you start the journey back to connecting to your full and complete self. It's great to have a starting point so you can look back and see how far you have come.

The wheel has wedges that represent eight major areas of your life: Family and Friends, Career, Money, Health, Physical Environment, Personal Growth/Spirituality, Fun and Recreation, and Significant Other/Romance. When you fill it out, you will have a simple graphic depicting how you feel you are doing in all these areas right now, before your journey begins.

The center of the wheel represents the number zero. The outside edge of the wheel represents the number 10. You do the exercise by rating yourself on this scale from 1 to 10 as to how satisfied you are in each area. Then you pencil in a mark like a curve of a wheel at the place within each slice where your number sits.

Wheel of Life Sample

The example on the next page is the Wheel of Life one of my clients filled out. Because she felt very satisfied with her Physical Environment and her Health, she ranked it high. But, her satisfaction level was quite a bit lower in the areas of Family & Friends and Significant Other/Romance, so they got a lower rating. She felt guilty about not spending enough time with her family and friends. She also noticed that she accommodated a lot for her husband and was trying to please everyone. That was why her scores were low in those two areas.

She stayed at home with her children so she used the Career wedge to represent that area of her life. Even though she felt extreme highs and lows in that job, she averaged her satisfaction out to be somewhere in the middle.

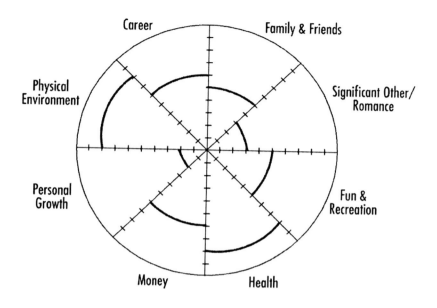

Money was also in the middle because she missed the feeling of earning "her own" money. But, her husband was well paid and they had good communication about finances. As such, the middle level seemed right to her.

She spent some time having fun but it was primarily to entertain her children. She didn't really have fun just for herself so she rated the Fun & Recreation wedge low.

Personal Growth was a tough one for her. It was difficult to admit, but she was feeling a little empty. She also felt that she was so devoted to her children that she was not very good at nurturing herself. She felt like she'd lost her old self. So, to be honest, and in an attempt to make the most of the process, Personal Growth ended up being her lowest satisfaction area.

Like the above example, your Wheel of Life will probably not be a perfect circle because each area will be a different number. The purpose of this exercise is to survey your level of satisfaction. You can then see what areas need more attention. As you work on them, your level of satisfaction will rise. Your goal is to move towards a large and perfect circle because that will feel like a more balanced and fulfilling life.

Exercise: Fill Out the Wheel of Life

Take a few minutes now to fill out your own version of the Wheel of Life.

You can download your own blank copy of the Wheel of Life at www.mothersonfire.com.

Exercise: Empowering Questions About Your Wheel of Life

What is the Wheel of Life telling you? How do you feel about your life? Below you will find some powerful coaching questions. Jot them down in your journal. Take time to reflect on your answers. There is no rush. You might want to take a few minutes each day with a cup of coffee or tea to reflect on one question at a time. Make this as easy as possible. Avoid putting pressure on yourself to get this done.

+ What do you think about your Wheel of Life?

+ What is it telling you about your life right now?

✦ What feelings is it bringing up?

✦ What is missing?

✦ What is working?

✦ What is surprising?

✦ What needs to change?

✦ What is your lowest area of satisfaction? Why is it low?

✦ What is your highest? Why is it high?

✦ Do these results reflect what is most important to you in your life?

✦ If you could change one area first, which area would it be?

✦ If your Wheel of Life were the wheel of a bicycle, how smooth or bumpy would the ride be?

✦ Is that what your life feels like—smooth or bumpy?

✦ If you had to share this wheel with a friend, what would you say about it?

EXERCISE: SHARE YOUR FINDINGS

Share your Wheel of Life with a friend! Who will it be and when?

The Wheel of Life is like a map.

But, it is only a map. There is much more to your experiences than what a number can say, yet there is lots to learn from this simple exercise. Many mothers are not surprised to see how lopsided their lives are. They know it in their hearts. But, it is something else to see it staring them in the face.

When mothers fill out the wheel honestly, their inner life flows out onto the page and is there to see in black and white. It says: *You are here! This is your life.*

To find fulfillment and build your inner fire, you need to face the reality of your life today. It's not always pleasant to do this. The good news is that as you work to complete yourself and build your inner fire, your Wheel of Life will change with you. One day you will do another Wheel of Life and see just how far you have come. Your rankings will reflect your growing sense of satisfaction and fulfillment.

We will be using this wheel again when we start to set goals, but for now, we are going to return to our fire metaphor and start looking for the spark that will help you to reconnect with yourself and ignite your inner fire.

CHAPTER FIVE: SUMMARY

✦ The Wheel of Life is a tool that helps you to get a general idea of where you are starting from and what you are working on with your personal growth journey.

✦ Just like a bicycle wheel with a flat tire, your Wheel of Life shows you how bumpy or smooth your life is going depending on how high or low your level of satisfaction is in the key areas of your life.

✦ Reflecting on your Wheel of Life will give you a good idea of the areas in your life that require more attention.

✦ Your goal is to move towards a Wheel of Life that looks like a large and unbroken circle because that will represent a more balanced and fulfilling life.

✦ The good news is that your inner fire—that flame of passion for life that you are building—exists right now within your life, in the very wheel that you just depicted.

6

FINDING YOUR INNER SPARK

*If you are distressed by anything external,
the pain is not due to the thing itself, but to
your own estimate of it; and this you have
the power to revoke at any moment.*

—Marcus Aurelius, Roman Emperor, 161–180 CE

STEP THREE:
PAY ATTENTION TO YOUR FEELINGS AND RECONNECT WITH YOUR NEEDS

Feelings, or emotions, are the energy of your life. Some psychologists call them "energy in motion." To feel more complete, you need to make emotions your friend. Why? Because they are the energy that will provide you with the spark that helps you light your inner fire and keep it burning.

Motherhood brings out many emotions. You can go from feeling immense joy and pride to deep guilt or shame, sometimes within the span of a few minutes. Sometimes mothers try to ignore or "get over" their feelings rather than acknowledge them and learn from them. As a result, they can feel numb or empty inside. To ignore or bottle up emotions can also cause stress and frustration. Many of us don't realize how this disconnection from our underlying emotions causes several of the daily irritations we feel.

In addition, when a mother thinks about changing things and trying to feel more complete and happy, this focus on herself brings up feelings of guilt, frustration, and obligation. Adjusting to motherhood can be such an emotional roller-coaster ride that we might just want to sometimes shut down and get off.

I am sure you have noticed that other people can misunderstand your emotions. In truth, we also misunderstand them ourselves. We don't always know why we are feeling the way we do, and we don't always know how to feel better when we are feeling bad. As I mentioned above, when we are feeling bad, some of us try to push the feelings away. Some of us eat something comforting or even overeat to soothe ourselves. In extreme cases, people turn to drugs or alcohol to try to change their moods and cope with difficult feelings.

Positive feelings are easier for most people to handle. The problem is, most of us don't feel them enough. Extremely positive feelings can even derail some people too. This misunderstanding of our emotions can drain us. We lose our spark for life.

EMOTIONS 101
Emotions hold a message for you.
To feel complete, we need to adopt a positive perspective on our emotions. Our emotions are like messengers. They tell us

when our needs are being met and when they are not being met. For example, if I need some attention and I don't get it, I feel angry. But if I do get it, I feel relaxed and happy. If I need food because I am hungry and I can't find something I like to eat, I feel frustrated and I get cranky. But if I need food and there is something nourishing at hand, I feel satisfied and relaxed. Is this sounding familiar? Doesn't this sound like your children?

Well, as a wise colleague of mine likes to say, *We are only children with longer legs!* The important thing to understand about our emotions is that they can lead us to our needs. For mothers this is critical, because mothers are geniuses at figuring out what everyone else needs, but not so good at paying attention to their own needs.

EXERCISE: CONNECTING EMOTIONS TO YOUR NEEDS

Humans all have basic needs that are linked to our physical well-being. But, we have emotional, spiritual, and intellectual needs also. Just like with children, when our needs are being met or not being met, we feel it as emotion.

1. For one week, start to connect your emotions to your needs. If you find yourself getting angry, ask yourself what need is *not* being met in this situation or relationship. When you are feeling peaceful or inspired or happy, ask yourself what needs *are* being met. Record this in your journal.

2. At the end of the week, take a look back at what you've written to see if you can identify some common themes. For example, does the need for "order" come up a lot? What about self-expression, intimacy, or clarity?

3. Also note what your energy is like when your needs are not being met and when they are. Having unmet needs will bring you down. Your life spark will be faint. Having your needs met, however, energizes you. You have a more powerful spark, not from anger or frustration, but from the sense of satisfaction and well-being that comes when your needs are met. It is very difficult to focus on living from the longing of your soul when your needs are not being met.

As you reflect on your needs, you will be getting more and more in touch with yourself. You will probably find that your top needs are the ones that keep appearing in your journal repeatedly. Now you have a good idea of what your personal needs are.

You can continue to deepen your connection with yourself by asking this question: When this need is met, will it lead to any other needs being met? For example, if the need for order keeps coming up, what other needs might be met when order is fulfilled? You may find out that your need for order is actually your need for safety or security or even power. This is how you can get down to your core needs. Now you can focus on meeting those core needs also.

Sometimes I meet mothers who have cut themselves off from their feelings so completely that they really don't feel them. If I ask them what they are feeling, they just go blank. If this has happened to you, start the journey back to your feelings by paying attention to the physical sensations in your body. Emotions flow like energy in your body. Notice what sensations are in your stomach area or solar plexus. Check in with your shoulders and hips. How about your head? Do you have headaches or tingling?

Eventually, as you connect more with these physical sensations, you can put language to them. For example, when there is a tightness in your throat, you might be able to identify that with feeling shut down by someone, or afraid of something. You will start to feel your feelings more and more. Then you can follow them to your needs. Once you let your feelings flow, you will find you have more spark for life, the spark you need to light your inner fire.

Needs List

Recognizing, acknowledging, and then meeting your needs are fundamental skills for helping you connect to yourself. Below is a list of many human needs to help you identify your own needs while you work through the above exercise.

Needs are neither good nor bad—they just are.
You will start to feel more yourself as you recognize your needs. But, be alert to the tendency to discount them or judge them. Needs are neither good nor bad, they are just a

Needs List

CONNECTION
acceptance
affection
appreciation
belonging
cooperation
communication
closeness
community
companionship
compassion
consideration
consistency
empathy
inclusion
intimacy
love
mutuality
nurturing
respect/self-respect
safety
security
stability
support
to know and be known
to see and be seen
to understand and be understood
trust
warmth

PHYSICAL WELL-BEING
air
food
movement/exercise
rest/sleep
sexual expression
safety
shelter
touch
water

HONESTY
authenticity
integrity
presence

PLAY
joy
humor

PEACE
beauty
communion
ease
equality
harmony
inspiration
order

MEANING	MEANING *(continued)*
awareness	mourning
celebration of life	participation
challenge	purpose
clarity	self-expression
competence	stimulation
consciousness	to matter
contribution	understanding
creativity	
discovery	AUTONOMY
efficacy	choice
effectiveness	freedom
growth	independence
hope	space
learning	spontaneity

part of being human. Many of my clients worry that having needs makes them "needy," which has a negative connotation for them. They worry that some needs may make them seem selfish. Or for some, they think that having needs at all is a sign of weakness.

Having needs and being "needy" are different. All humans of every age and stage of life have needs. We only become "needy" when we expect or demand that other people meet them for us. Children are needy by nature. But, when we are adults, it is our responsibility to learn how to meet our own needs. So, if you have learned that "to matter" is one of your top needs, for example, then it is up to you to find ways to feel like you matter.

I knew one mother who would feel deeply hurt at dinner time when her family would sit down to eat without a word of thanks or enthusiasm. At first, she sat quietly, feeling badly, but rationalized it by telling herself that this was the role of mother and wife and that needing thanks was selfish and wrong and that it was a sign of insecurity.

Through coaching, she began to accept that her need was neither good nor bad and that she had a right to try to meet it. At first, she just got angry, thinking that they should know better and she still said nothing. Then finally, she sat down with her family one night at the table and told them how she felt. She shared with them that she needed to be acknowledged and appreciated for her time shopping and cooking for them. She did not like feeling taken for granted. She even said what she wanted—to be thanked and told how much they appreciated her efforts before the family started eating.

And so they did. Sometimes, if they forgot, she was able to make a joke about it by standing up and bowing or pointing a finger at herself and laughing about how great she was.

She took responsibility for her needs by asking for what she wanted. She no longer expected her family to just magically meet her needs; instead, she paid attention to her feelings, figured out what she needed, and then asked for it. She may have needed their cooperation, but they were happy to give it to her especially because she was able to communicate her needs without anger or criticism. She also noticed that she had more energy and joy when she was food shopping and cooking. She got her spark back.

Mothers are reluctant to make their needs a priority.
The great gift of emotions is that they can point you to your needs, which, in turn, help you to reconnect to yourself again. Still, one of the obstacles mothers face with this step is their reluctance to make their own needs a priority; we talked about this earlier in the book. Mothers will bend over backwards to meet their commitments to others, yet they are willing to let themselves down. I see this with so many women. So, be easy on yourself and start with baby steps.

EXERCISE: MAKING YOUR NEEDS A PRIORITY

Pick one of your top needs and look at ways you can meet it more consistently. For example, if you discover that order is one of your top needs, determine something simple that would help you to meet that need. Is it a better calendar for writing things down? Is it taking something off your plate to reduce the chaos? Is it getting things ready the night before to minimize the morning craziness? Is it hiring a professional organizer to help you declutter your home or just having a friend come over to help?

Taking care of your needs feels good.

Let yourself enjoy the benefits of taking care of yourself by meeting your needs. Many women are surprised to discover how easy it is to meet some of their needs. Small and easy changes like having someone acknowledge your dinner efforts or giving yourself the gift of getting help to organize can add up to a much happier life. You will see how quickly your spark for life comes back.

Some people may complain.

Don't be deterred if people start to complain. They are not used to you taking care of yourself. When you start to change the status quo, they will have to learn to meet some of their needs themselves also! But, a little self-reliance never hurt anybody. Your family and friends will adjust, and one of the benefits will be that you will become emotionally more balanced and energized. You will feel your inner fire warming and lighting up everyone.

Needs lead you to what you want.

Once you get more connected to your needs, you can then get clarity on what you want. I have mentioned before that some of the mothers I coach start off not really knowing what they want. They may know what they *don't* want, but are having difficulty pinpointing what it is they *do* want. They have come to coaching because of a vague feeling of needing more ... but what is that "more"?

What you want is what it takes to meet your needs. You might want to read that sentence again. It's simple, but powerful. *What you want is what it takes to meet your needs.* For example, one of my clients came to coaching because she felt a little empty. She loved her family and staying at home with her children, but something was missing and she just couldn't figure it out. She really thought being a mother should have been enough.

As she started to pay more attention to her feelings, she noticed, as she reread her journal, that she felt a lot of pleasure and satisfaction decorating her home and helping her friends decorate theirs. We identified that creativity was one of her core needs. To meet that need, she realized that she *wanted* to go back and finish a college certificate in design that she had started before she had her second child. And so, one night a week, she traveled downtown and eventually completed the course. She figured out what she wanted by sorting out what would meet her need for creativity.

All through the process, I noticed how the spark came back into her eyes when she talked about what she was learning. She would get so excited. She shared her experiences with her family. She was enjoying herself.

This client's process seems very neat and easy when it is written down on paper. But, in reality, connecting with what she wanted took her many months. She had some stops and starts. She wasn't quite sure which need was the "right" need to fill her emptiness. In fact, she saw it as many different needs. But, with baby steps, she worked it through in her journal as well as by talking it over in her coaching group.

Eventually, she knew the need for creativity was right because she felt good whenever she was doing creative things. By paying attention to how she felt, she was able to reconnect with herself on the level of her needs and the end result was a Mother on Fire.

EMOTIONS 201
Our thinking affects our emotions.

It is part of the way people are wired that we react emotionally when our needs are met or not met. Our thoughts can play a role in our emotions as well. For example, when I am feeling down and depleted, I notice how I start to think negatively about everything—*I'll never be successful enough ... No one understands me ... I really messed up ... I am such a pain ... They are such a pain!*

So, which came first, my generalized negativity or my low feelings? Well, if a need of mine is not being met, I start to feel low and then my mind jumps in with its two cents on how bad everything else is and before too long, I am lying on the couch, watching television, eating chips and numbing out!

We've met those negative thought processes before: it's our inner critic. Just like it can thwart us from beginning our journey of personal fulfillment, the inner critic can come up with lots of reasons for us to feel bad in general. That inner voice of negativity really dampens our energy and spark for life. In Chapter Three, we talked about how change requires a shift in thinking. That level of attention to thinking is required here, too, if your needs are to be met successfully.

Unless you are clinically depressed and would therefore benefit from seeking medical help, your moods will pass. Emotions, as I said at the start of this chapter, are energy in motion. They tend to stick around only when we grab onto them like a dog with a bone and chew on them for hours.

Unfortunately, when we generalize our negativity, sometimes we get too down and too depleted to take the action we might need for meeting our needs. And so, it is very useful to learn how to switch from the negative spiraling into a more positive and productive state of mind. Once your mood has changed and you feel more balanced, you can look for the message or the learning within the experience.

There is power in positive thinking.

Likely, you have heard about the idea of positive thinking. You might even have an opinion about it. Some people have the wrong idea about positive thinking. They think it's about taking a bad situation and pretending it's okay, rather like pouring pink paint over garbage. But, that isn't the true idea of positive thinking.

Positive thinking is a skill you can use to help you to get your thinking back in perspective. It is a change in your focus. As you read earlier, when you are caught in a negative spiral, you are seeing only one perspective, the negative one. But, life isn't that simple. There are always more perspectives.

And so, the skill of positive thinking is actually the skill of shifting your focus, which allows you to slowly but surely get a more balanced perspective.

A positive focus improves your mood.

Changing your focus from negative to positive has a profound effect on your mood. For example, I was walking on a downtown city sidewalk on a quiet Sunday morning during a snowstorm, when a large, noisy, and somewhat scary-looking snowplow came onto the sidewalk to clear it. First, I got irritated by the noise and fumes. Then I got angry at how aggressive the driver seemed by not slowing down when he saw me. Finally, I got really upset when I had to move out of the way. I saw the driver was young and I had negative thoughts about him, too. It was only a moment earlier that I was enjoying the walk. In seconds, I was in a bad mood. My life spark was buried under a lot of crankiness!

As the machine passed, I stopped myself. I didn't want to feel bad. I realized that my needs for peace and safety were being compromised. That was probably why I reacted. But, I looked at how clear the sidewalk was. I started to list all the positive aspects:

> *I love that I live in such a prosperous city that they clear the sidewalks on downtown streets. I love how that young man has a job. I love that I don't have to worry about my footing. And I love how quickly the peace of the moment was restored. I love that I live downtown and*

can walk everywhere. I love the look of the buildings. And I love that it's Sunday and I have a day off work to enjoy.

After a few of those thoughts, my mood went right back to enjoying my walk.

EXERCISE: IDENTIFYING THE POSITIVE ASPECTS OF A SITUATION

Now it's your turn. Use your journal to record the positive aspects of situations that upset you or that are not going well. For example, if you have a day where the dependency of your child is really getting to you, list some of the positive aspects of your relationship.

Write out things that make you feel a little bit of relief, thoughts that make you feel better. You are not pretending that the negative isn't there—you are just refocusing your attention. For example, you could write about how you know this situation will pass. Remember the moments when she is happy and playing well. Think about the ways she has grown. Think about how quickly children grow. Find something else to focus on, like her laugh, her love of her stuffed animals, the way she lights up when she sees her grandparents. Think about the moments when you two are playing well together, when you are happy and enjoying her company.

You can also use this exercise to write about the things you are already enjoying in your life in general and in your other relationships. This really strengthens your skill of finding positive aspects and can be truly pleasurable.

It seems that people can easily chew on the bone of what they don't like or want or feel bad about. To improve your mood is harder. But, it is a habit like any other. The more you practice it, the better you get at it and before too long, you will be able to manage your moods.

Making your needs a priority and learning how to meet them will help you to reconnect to yourself. This connection with your needs and emotions can be like an internal GPS, guiding you to go in the direction of what feels better.

And, because your emotions are energy in motion, your new skills of managing your moods, learning to find relief, and feeling better will raise you up and put the spark back into your life. You will be able to sustain the energy, focus, and interest needed to pursue a more fulfilled life and become a Mother on Fire.

CHAPTER SIX: SUMMARY

+ Your feelings or emotions are the energy of your life.

+ Ignoring your feelings can cause stress and frustration.

+ Your emotions can also lead you to your needs by noticing what needs are being met (or not met) when you feel a certain way.

+ Your needs are neither good nor bad, they are just part of being human.

+ You are the only person responsible and capable of meeting your own needs.

✦ Your thinking also affects your emotions.

✦ Use the skill of positive thinking by learning how to shift your focus from a negative to a positive perspective in any situation.

✦ Making your needs a priority and learning how to meet them will help you to reconnect with yourself.

7

Making Sure Your Inner Fire Expresses Your Authentic Self

It's easy to say "no!" when there's a deeper "yes!" burning inside.

—Stephen Covey, author

Step Four: Identify and Live By Your Core Values

In Step Three, you found the spark you need to light your inner fire by reconnecting with your emotions in a meaningful way and identifying your needs and wants. But, you want to make sure you are lighting an inner fire that is an expression of you—the true, authentic you, rather than the reflection of the expectations or ideas that belong to others. So, in Step Four, you will learn how to identify and live by your core values. Your values are the kindling you will need to support your inner fire.

Needs, wants, and values—these all point to *you*, the parts of you that you may have lost during the lifestyle and emotional changes of motherhood. Reconnecting with them is key to feeling complete, and living the life of a Mother on Fire.

Core values are the principles that are most fundamental to you.

My clients often tell me that they start to enjoy their lives more once they've begun to honor their core values. Instead of losing themselves by molding and adapting to everyone else's ideas, they feel they are living with more integrity because they are respecting their values. When you honor your core values while you fulfill your role as a mother, you feel more harmonious and complete.

The way you define and organize your core values makes you unique. They are like fingerprints: no two people's values are exactly alike. Even if you share a value such as love, the way each of us defines that concept, feels the emotions associated with it, or acts on it, is different and unique. You are an original now and for eternity. No matter how much you may have conformed to expectations, underneath it all, there will never be anyone quite like you. Don't you just love that about yourself?

Knowing your core values has huge benefits.

If you are not fully connected to and living from your core values, you may be finding that life is a struggle. Perhaps making decisions is difficult as you deal with conflicting needs and wants. Perhaps you are striving to please others only to find you are not happy. Or, maybe your daily activities lack a sense of purpose beyond the tasks associated with being a mother.

Connecting with your core values can bring more ease

into your life. Using values as your guide gives structure to your decision-making because you can measure your choices against your values. Instead of worrying endlessly about the right decision by other people's standards or by what you've been conditioned to think, you can look to see which decision best honors your values. It is like having a personal checklist; the better the match, the better you will feel and the more confidence you will have in your choices.

One of my clients, a stay-at-home mother, found herself consumed by and perhaps a little over-invested in her youngest child. He was very dependent on her, too. Part of her loved that. But, she was also feeling a little stir crazy and crowded at times. This pull on her evoked feelings of guilt and confusion.

She remembered how she had really valued her independence and alone time before she had children and realized that this was probably one of her core values, but a strong instinct was pulling her the other way. She didn't actually feel a desire for freedom directly, or wish to force independence on her son. She also valued the closeness she had with her son highly. She was experiencing a growing sense of irritation without the motivation to change anything. After the exercise of identifying her core values, she determined that most likely, her value of independence was being compromised even as her other value of closeness was being met.

What should she do? Her values seemed to be competing and conflicting with each other. Should she force herself to break free even without the motivation to do so—and even though her instincts were guiding her the other way—in order to rekindle her desire for independence?

She wasn't sure, but she began to think the answer might be yes. Even if it broke her heart in the process and was hard on everybody involved, taking steps to do this might ultimately teach or condition her child to have some independence while at the same time give her space to reconnect with herself. Practically speaking, we discussed many possibilities—for example, enrolling her child in part-time day care, even if she wasn't working, or setting a time each week to leave the house so that someone else was in charge of the daily routines. The idea was that perhaps one day, taking some time for herself would no longer be a struggle, and if it was no longer a struggle, she might actually start to feel an urge to do it—therefore allowing her to honor her value of independence again.

So she started to take more time for herself. At first, it was emotionally hard on her. Even baby steps challenged her. She started by taking time in the evening several times a week to journal. She had to go to her bedroom, shut the door and explain to her youngest who cried and came knocking, that she had a little work to do and to go to daddy. She said it was really tough to not just give in, and that sometimes her son would cry for the whole time she was in there.

But, she found that with time her son got used to the new routine and that her alone time became so energizing and pleasurable that she stopped feeling so pulled or guilty. Over time, she learned more ways to honor all her values, not all at the same time, but in a balanced and realistic way. One of the results was totally unexpected. On one weekend a few years after she started this process, she took a weekend away to attend a personal growth coaching workshop. She had never done that before. Over the years, though, she and her family had become accepting of her need to honor her values and some of the new behaviors that stemmed from these values.

And so, on this particular weekend away, her husband took the children, including their youngest, to a basketball game, played with them at the house, and even took them to his buddy's house to hang out with him and his children. Everyone had a great time and while she was honoring her values, her husband was having a chance to bond and enjoy the children in a way that was different than when she was around. It turned out to be a win-win for all involved. As well, her youngest was learning independence from mommy.

Knowing your core values is motivating.
There are hidden benefits to living from your values also. Mothers who are in the habit of procrastinating find that when they focus deliberately on the values they are honoring with their activities, they ease into them more quickly and enjoy them more. They feel motivated because, by linking their activities to their values, the activities seem more meaningful. They also start to let go of some of the activities that are not linked to their values. There is an inherent pleasure in living in tune with your values.

You can use your values in tandem with your emotions as another source of energy for your life. They are the kindling that is always burning underneath your fire. Instead of always reacting to the enormous quantities of stimuli in the world, you look within yourself for guidance. In other words, your authentic self becomes your source for direction, motivation, inspiration, and energy.

Practice giving yourself permission to say NO to the activities that are not honoring your values and YES to those that do. I bet that those activities that don't support your values are the things that drain you and prevent you from really enjoying the activities that do support your authentic self.

Honoring your core values is not always easy.

Honoring your values, like most processes of personal growth, can be tough, messy, and not always progressive in a linear fashion. Remember: baby steps. As you learn to ground your decisions and activities in your values in a conscious and deliberate way, your life will feel even more purposeful and directed.

You want your inner fire to be an expression of your core values so that you are staying true to yourself and not getting lost in the ideas, demands, expectations, or values of others.

DISCOVER YOUR VALUES

In the exercise below, you are going to discover your values by exploring something called a *peak experience*. The term peak experience originated with the psychologists Carl Rogers and Abraham Maslow. Maslow used the phrase to describe nonreligious experiences that are accompanied by strong feelings of happiness and well-being, and the sense that everything is right. Maslow influenced the science of psychology by proposing something that seems obvious to us today—that even though people have depression and anxiety in their lives, they are also quite capable of experiencing joy and fulfillment. He also noted that some people were particularly skilled at having those peak experiences. No matter what our lives have been like in general, there are usually moments, even fleeting ones, where we've had a peak experience.

Part of what makes them peak experiences is that, in those moments, you are living from your authentic self and fulfilling your core values. And so, if you work at discovering what elements were present in those peak experiences, you can produce a word description of your core values. Identifying those elements will help you to reconnect with your authentic self again.

EXERCISE: VALUES CLARIFICATION

1. Think of a time, even if it is just a moment, when you felt fulfilled, when life was really good. It might have been a sense that all was right with the world. It might have felt like a deep sense of inner peace or extreme joy. I often have these peak moments after a yoga class. As I am walking home, I get a rush through me and I think, "Wow, this is the greatest day of my life!" That is a momentary peak experience.

2. Write down your peak experiences in your journal. Do your best to make sure it's a peak experience you really felt and not something you think you were supposed to feel. For example, some women in my workshops have written down their wedding day or the birth of their first child, then realized this was because they felt those moments *should* be peak experiences even if they were not. You can have great experiences without them being a peak experience. You want to reconnect to those times when you felt a very deep contentment. Your wedding day and the birth of a child might be a peak experience for you or it might not have been. Be as honest with yourself as possible.

Also, I have had clients who really could not find any such experience. If that is happening for you, then just make it up. In other words, what would be a peak experience for you? Have you always dreamed of walking on a beach in Hawaii at sunset with your dog? If so, you would use that as your peak experience.

Here are some examples from several of my coaching clients:

+ Riding my bicycle into the grounds of the university in the fall

+ Walking in the woods

+ Closing a very important deal at work

+ Climbing a mountain in Europe

+ Watching my child walk for the first time

+ Trying snowboarding for the first time

+ Going to live music concerts

+ Feeling the sun on my skin while relaxing on the dock at my family cottage on a very hot summer day

+ Dinner with my whole extended family on special occasions

+ Hearing my baby's laughter

3. Review your peak experience and distill the values that you were experiencing at the time. Were you experiencing a lot of nurturing or adventure? Then nurturing or adventure may be core values for you. Perhaps you were having a really good laugh. In that case, "sense of humor" or "joy" might be one of your core values. Think of your values as the feelings you were experiencing at the time. You may have been with your family, but what were you feeling? Did you have a strong sense of duty, or was it a powerful feeling of belonging? In that case, "duty" or "belonging" would be your values.

My yoga example points to my values of spirituality and freedom.

4. Peak experiences often reflect what Eckhart Tolle describes as "being present" in his books *A New Earth* and *The Power of Now*. They are the moments when we are able to get out of our incessant thinking and judging and instead simply *be* in the moment. This way of thinking ties into my earlier

explanation of human *beings* versus human *doings*. What were the values you were experiencing in that present moment of your peak experience? Don't worry if you find an overlap. Write them down in your journal.

Here are some of the values (in italics) that my clients identified in the examples above.

+ Riding my bicycle into the grounds of the university in the fall
  – *learning*

+ Walking in the woods
  – *closeness to nature, spirituality, solitude*

+ Closing a very important deal at work
  – *achievement, success, prosperity, recognition*

+ Climbing a mountain in Europe
  – *physical challenge, sharing experiences with others, adventure*

+ Watching my child walk for the first time
  – *connection, achievement, joy*

+ Trying snowboarding for the first time
  – *risk, thrills, fun, adventure*

+ Going to live music concerts
  – *fun, independence, creativity*

✦ Feeling the sun on my skin while relaxing on the dock at my family cottage on a very hot summer day
  – *connection with others, closeness, simplicity*

✦ Dinner with my whole extended family on special occasions
  – *tradition, fun*

✦ My baby's laughter
  – *caring for others, joy, attachment, nurturing*

On the next page is a list of more values to help you in case you get stuck for the right word.

5. Review your list and see if you can either increase it or reduce it to five values. If you have more than that, you can reduce it by combining some of them to make a value string. If you have "caring" and "giving" and "nurturing" on your list, you could combine them into a string. Pick the primary word, the word that describes the main feeling for you to head the string. For example, "nurturing/giving/caring" or "zest for life/enthusiasm/energy/fun."

6. Creating a value string helps you to further refine your values. The words you put together act like a fingerprint of your authentic self. Many people will have the value of caring, but it is unlikely that two people will have identical value strings. Because each feeling means something different to each person, the words you include in your string will help to make your values list unique to you.

Values List

accomplishment/results	intimacy
achievement	justice and fairness
acknowledgment	leadership
adventure/excitement	learning
altruism	leaving a legacy
authenticity	to love and be loved
autonomy	loyalty
beauty	magic
belonging	mastery
clarity	nature
commitment	openness
community	orderliness
completion	partnership
connecting	peace
creativity	personal growth
making a difference	power
emotional health	privacy
enthusiasm	recognition
environment	risk taking
excellence	romance
experience and create joy	security
freedom	self-expression
fun	sensuality
giving	spirituality
helping	spontaneity
honesty	trust
humor	variety
influencing others	vitality
integrity	zest for life

Here is an example based on my peak experiences of yoga, coaching, and visiting some friends and family in California:

◆ spirituality/inner peace/presence

◆ transformation/living my potential/helping others to live their potential

◆ creativity/beauty in my surroundings

◆ to love and be loved/connection with people

◆ freedom

Write out your value strings in your journal, in no particular order.

Live Your Values

In order to change things in our lives, we need to be aware of what we are changing. Now that you know about your core values, reflecting on a day in your life will raise your awareness around how you are living your values and how you are not.

EXERCISE: REFLECTING ON YOUR DAY

Review your day or week—whenever you can do this—and list the times you were living your values. Use your journal to write down your reflections. For example, if I went to a yoga class, I would write that down. Write about how you felt. Keep your focus on the positive as much as possible.

If you find yourself writing about something that did not feel good, see if you can identify the value that this situation or activity was not honoring. Write about what you would have liked instead. Here's an example from one of my journal entries.

> *I had a lovely dinner at my friend's house tonight. I really enjoyed myself. I was definitely honoring my value of connection. But, I was really irritated before I left my place. Hmm. I needed more time for sure so I called to say I would be late. I think I was honoring my value of freedom when I did that because then I felt free to do what I needed and wanted to do before I got there. I wasn't constrained by her time frame. It worked out really well. I appreciated her flexibility. She's a great friend.*

Soon, you will start to reflect on your values before you take action or make a decision. That way, you can decide whether to do something or even act a certain way before you do it. In time, you will find that you are making more and more choices that keep you in alignment with your core values. You will begin to feel more and more yourself, your authentic self. Now you can be sure that your life and your inner fire are true to you. You are becoming a Mother on Fire.

CHAPTER SEVEN: SUMMARY

+ Your values are the kindling you need to support your inner fire.

+ The way you define and organize your core values makes you unique.

* Connecting to your core values brings more ease into your life.

* The activities in your life become more meaningful when they are linked to your values.

* The peak experience exercise helps you to reconnect with your values.

* Taking the time to reflect on a day in your life will raise your awareness around how you are currently living your values and how you are not.

8

FUELING YOUR FIRE

*We must look for ways to become an
active force in our own lives.
We must take charge of our own destinies,
design a life of substance.*

—Les Brown, motivational speaker

STEP FIVE: SET GOALS

As ethereal and dreamy as the quest for personal fulfillment can sometimes get, at its bottom line it is about setting and achieving goals. Not just any goals, of course. To live from the longing of your soul, your goals need to really resonate. You need to feel them excite you within.

Meaningful goals connect to your core values.

In order for your life to be fulfilling, it must include the expression of your core values. In contrast, basing your life too much on what you think you *should* be, have, or do can lead to disappointment, frustration, and a sense of inadequacy or emptiness.

Moreover, living a life that is not truly an expression of your authentic self is not powerful. It has little positive energy and often results in an inner struggle that drains and weakens you. Doubts overwhelm. It is very stressful. And, as a result, fulfillment is either not attainable or sustainable. This is why the goals you set must be aligned with your core values. That way your goals will be meaningful to you because they are authentic and leading you towards feeling more fulfilled and complete.

THE VISION
Meaningful goals connect to your life vision.
For goals to resonate and excite you, they also need to connect you to your life vision.

Life vision? you say. *What is that?*

Your life vision is what your life might look like when all the wedges of your Wheel of Life from Chapter Five are rated at a 10—a full-out expression of everything you desire. Your vision expresses those deeply held desires that I have called the longing of your soul. Your vision is like the North Star; it gives you a reference point to guide you toward your fulfillment. It is also like the horizon line. As long as you are alive, your vision will keep growing and moving forward, showing you more—more of the things you love to do, more about the person you enjoy being, more experiences that excite and fulfill you.

The vision you have for your life is your dream life. And, as fanciful as that sounds, your dream life can be realized. It takes commitment, understanding, and consistently setting and achieving goals that point in its direction.

Exercise: Creating a Life Vision

1. Put on some music and dance. Yes, you read that right. Before you sit down to think about your vision, I want you to *not* think about it first. Put on your inspirational music from Step One. Or, dance to music you remember from your youth. Find several songs that really make you want to move.

   I have noticed that many moms I coach are a little tightly wound. They have so many responsibilities that feel so burdensome that their spontaneity and *joie de vivre* are compromised. By getting up and just dancing as if no one is watching, you loosen up your creativity. The vision you create after you are loose will have a lot of positive energy and enthusiasm in it.

2. Take out your journal and flip back to the Wheel of Life you filled out in Step Two. Go around each wedge and start to write out what each wedge would look like if it were at a 10 right now and in the future. What are the elements that would make it a 10 for you? Let it flow. This is brainstorming. You can edit it later if need be.

   For example: If your "Significant Other/Romance" wedge was rated at a three, a 10 might look like more and better communication, romantic dates, time alone, a vacation without children, more sex, more family time that is just fun, feeling closer, less anger on your part, and more appreciation.

Once you have gone around the whole wheel, you now have a life vision. Your vision is the image of your inner fire fully formed. The goals you will set in the next exercise are the branches that will fuel it.

THE GOALS

Setting goals is powerful.

I cannot stress enough the power of goal-setting. Our minds are goal-directed machines. Getting up and dressed in the morning are goals. Getting the children awake, dressed, and out the door on time are goals. These are the often unconscious goals of our everyday life.

When you are striving to feel more complete, connected to yourself, and committed to your personal fulfillment, setting goals helps you become more conscious and active in designing your life, instead of letting it "just happen."

Setting goals gives your life direction.

> Most people spend more time planning their
> vacations than they do planning their lives.
> —financial planning ad

Setting goals is the foundation of a life plan designed to fulfill your vision. Mothers tend to be very skilled at planning for the family, but somehow they forget to set meaningful goals and plans for themselves.

Without conscious, meaningful goals that are connected to your values and vision, you can sometimes feel as directionless as a piece of driftwood, bobbing along in the great sea of life. Meaningful goals help you to get the most out of your life, just as having financial goals helps you to get the most out of your money. Instead of aimlessly wishing for things to be different, goals give you a focus and a direction you can follow with confidence because you have chosen them for yourself so you are not always at the mercy of others' needs or even your own sense of obligation.

Goals give your task list more meaning.

Goals also help you to keep your endless task list in check. Ideally, tasks will either come out of your goals or link back to them. Because your goals are in alignment with your core values and leading to your vision, you can stay connected to your authentic self and your personal fulfillment as you perform your tasks. For example, even if you are doing laundry or helping your child with homework, if you are aware of a connection between your tasks and your goals, core values, and vision, they become as much for you as for other people.

Mothers often feel frustrated when their tasks seem endless and thankless. For mothers who value their family life running smoothly or need things like order and harmony, they can connect their tasks with their needs, goals, values, and vision. That can help reduce their frustration.

I have also coached some mothers for whom those household chores are just not meaningful. They don't actually need or value that kind of order, but rather value spontaneity, for example. Once they realized that, they were able to relax when the house was a little chaotic. They stopped driving themselves crazy trying to create something that just wasn't that important to them.

You can keep your task list in check by making sure your tasks have some meaning for you and giving yourself permission to lighten up on those that don't.

Okay? Let's Goal!

EXERCISE: SETTING MEANINGFUL GOALS AROUND THE WHEEL OF LIFE

With your vision and your Wheel of Life, you are ready to start setting meaningful goals.

1. Divide a page in your journal into three columns—*Wheel of Life*, *Goal*, and *Core Value*.

2. Pick one wedge of your wheel to work on at a time. Write the name of the wedge into the first column. Write the number you assigned to that wedge also.

3. You know that your vision for that wedge is a 10, so ask yourself what would have to happen to move you closer to that 10. You can think of it in small increments if that helps. For example, if we use the example above, "Significant Other/Romance" was rated as a three. What would a four look like? Your vision has a lot to choose from. Could it be a planned date night every week or once a month? If so, write that down as your goal in column two.

Sample Goals List

WHEEL OF LIFE	GOAL	VALUE
Sig. Other/Romance – 3	Weekly date night	Connection
Career – 6	Stop yelling at children	Connection/harmony
Money – 7	Save a little for me	Autonomy/ independence
Physical Environment – 4	Sort and throw out magazines, toys	Order/harmony
Friends/Family – 5	Have coffee weekly with friends	Connection
Personal Growth – 4	Keep working on this book	Zest for life/vitality
Health – 8	Gym 3x a week	Zest for life/vitality
Fun/Recreation – 7	Go skiing 2x a year with kids	Zest for life/vitality

4. Complete this process for each wedge of the wheel.

5. Now let's go back and fill in column three—identify the value this goal aligns with. Refer back to your values list in Chapter Eight. Write down the value or value string that the goal is honoring. Do it for each of your goals. If you can't find a match, you have either missed a value the first time around or this goal is not an authentic one. It might be driven by your tendency to please or impress others, for example. It might be coming from a "should" rather than a true desire. If you need to, add a new value that

does resonate with you and your goal, or change the goal to something that does connect to a value.

6. Each time you achieve a goal, go back and set a new one. If you've made those date nights a habit, decide on the next goal that will move you toward that 10. Keep creating new charts, which will show your rankings rising higher and higher. Or, even fill out a new Wheel of Life every once in a while to see how your map is changing. Step by step, you will build on each small goal until one day you will realize that you are living your vision.

You are designing your life, no one else's.

One mother I coached who was working at a job she didn't really like, set a goal to seek a promotion. The promotion was part of her vision. But, when she looked for a value to connect it with, she couldn't find one. She realized that being promoted was not going to make her feel better at work. In fact, although she was a grown woman with children of her own, it was pressure from her parents that was motivating that goal.

When we went back to her vision and looked at her career wedge again, she started talking about leaving her job and finding a part-time position in a fun and hip yoga store. She loved visiting that store; its values resonated with her own. She talked about that store for several weeks to me and her coaching group. The idea really lit her up. Her inner flame was being fueled as she spoke of it.

Although she could not financially make the shift right away, she started to take small steps toward her ultimate vision. She set a goal to talk to her manager about initiating some flex hours at work. It took time to convince her, but eventually it happened. That moved her closer to her vision. While she was negotiating with her manager, she set another goal to spend some time at the yoga store talking to the staff and the manager. She enjoyed the feeling there, and connected with the people. She let them know she was interested in working there.

Finally, it happened: a part-time position opened up and they called her immediately. With her flex hours at work, she was able to take the job for a few hours a week.

All this change was not easy on her or her family. There were long discussions at home and difficult talks with her parents. Living a life based on your core values can be tough, especially when they conflict with others' values, but it is part of feeling complete—and necessary if you want the fire and positive energy to come back into your life.

It was important to my client to work on her vision and goals. It was a longing of her soul that wanted to be realized. Staying at her original job for financial reasons and status was not part of her ultimate vision. But, taking the steps to fulfill herself—even small ones—made her feel more alive and fueled her fire to keep striving to realize her ultimate vision.

The Motivation

Preventing overload

Chances are, you have set goals before and not reached them. That is true for everyone. There are a few things you can do to help you attain your goals.

Making sure they resonate with your values and connect to your vision is key. But, you also need to make sure you don't overload yourself. That can happen when you set goals that are just too big, or set too many at a time. Setting and achieving goals is a skill and it's best to start with things that seem doable right now. I call it taking the path of least resistance.

If your doubts and mental blocks create too much inner resistance to a goal, no matter how much it resonates, your resistant mindset will prevent you from achieving it. Find the path of least resistance by cutting the goal down to a more manageable size. You want to be able to say: "I can do that!"

If you are feeling some resistance now with any goal you have set, determine if it is too big. Maybe a date night each week is too much with all the other activities going on. You might feel tempted to just give up on it entirely when you can't get it together. Instead, figure out what you *can* do. Could you go out once a month? Or have a glass of wine together once in a while after the children are asleep? Could you take half an hour and connect without the television or the computer on?

Find your path of least resistance and do that. Do whatever you can do. Success breeds success. With each achievement you feel energized to keep going. That is how achieving a series of small, manageable goals leads to the accomplishment of something bigger—your vision.

It might help if you think of your goals as segments of your vision. The vision is the roaring fire. The goals are branches that can be chopped into manageable pieces. Throw one piece onto the fire at a time. Before you know it, the whole branch will be burning and you will feel the excitement and passion of living your vision and being on fire.

Accountability

Accountability is a key strategy in life coaching and really helps with motivation. When a client knows she has a coaching call or a meeting, she makes an extra effort to complete the items she committed to. Accountability really works. It is like having deadlines at a job or at school.

Find a way to set up some accountability for yourself. Ask one or more of your friends to hold you accountable. Better yet, form a group of other moms to work through this program. Check out the Mothers on Fire website and Forums for help with this at www.mothersonfire.com. If you can tell your friends about your goals and then check in with them, you are more likely to stay on track.

Reviewing

Oddly enough, sometimes we fail to achieve our goals because we forget about them. For example, you may write down your desire to spend romantic time with your husband and then forget about it! A month later as you look at your journal you realize it was there but forgotten. Good intentions often go unrealized simply because we get busy with other things.

To help you achieve your goals, review them regularly. I have several clients who read over their goals in bed on Sunday night. That way they can plan for some of them during the week. Other clients have written their goals on index cards and carry them around. Some put them on sticky notes and attach them to their bathroom mirrors. Computer-savvy moms have them on their computer and displayed where they can see them. Reviewing your goals is a simple action, yet very effective. Keeping your goals at the top of your mind will give you a much better chance of fulfilling them.

When the "goaling" gets tough.

I understand that as you read this chapter on goal setting, it might all sound too easy. The goal setting itself is easy. You're right. It is the goal *achievement* that can be tough. My client above who changed her work hours and found a part-time job at the yoga store made her changes over a period of time after she mustered the courage and commitment to face her manager, husband, and parents. There were times when she just wanted to dismiss her goal as stupid and unrealistic.

What will it take to make the changes, create the habits, and motivate yourself to work on your personal fulfillment? Research shows that people are motivated by two things—they are either moving toward something they want or moving away from something they don't want. When you find your motivation is lagging, as at times it surely will, try this exercise.

EXERCISE: IDENTIFYING WHAT YOU WANT AND DON'T WANT

1. Divide a page in your journal into two columns—*What I Want* and *What I Don't Want*.

2. Using the goal you are having trouble with, write out what the goal is, as specifically as possible, and then write out all the reasons why you want it. Being specific helps you to be clear on the details and perhaps even on the small steps to achieving the goal. Thinking about *why* you want it stirs up some emotions about the goal. Those emotions contain the positive energy and the spark you may be lacking. With your date night, for example, you could write out, *Every week I want us to have fun outside of the house. I want to start exploring all the restaurants in the neighborhood. Even if they are too expensive, we could just sit at the bar and have an appetizer or a cocktail. And why? I want to feel close to him again. I want our marriage to last and be a loving example to the kids. I love how I feel when we are connecting.*

3. Are you sufficiently pumped again? Now go over to the next column and write out everything you don't want related to that goal—the things you are moving away from and why you don't want them. If that pesky date night is not happening, write about what you are trying to change

WHAT I WANT: Date Night	WHAT I DON'T WANT: Distance
Be together once a week.	I don't want to always talk about the kids or his work because I get bored and shut down.
Check out the neighborhood restaurants.	
Talk about ourselves. Share our feelings. I want to feel closer.	I don't want this distance. We just seem to be drifting apart. That scares me.
Laugh and have fun. Get our mind off all the stress. I want our marriage to last. I want our kids to feel the love and closeness between us. I need the marriage relationship to be strong.	I don't want my indifference to him romantically. I seem to have lost my spark and I am too involved with the kids. I don't want our marriage to be like my parents'.

with that goal. *I don't want the distance I am feeling. I don't like how we only talk about the children or his work. I am afraid if this goes on for too long, we will lose affection for each other.*

4. When you are done journaling, talk to a friend about your goal. Ask her to hold you accountable to something, no matter how small. Make a plan to report in to her after it is done. Perhaps this friend could help you achieve this goal. If she agrees to babysit while you enjoy your date nights, for example, you can reciprocate with her children.

You can see from the above example that this exercise can get deep and emotional. The deeper you go with this, the more likely you will get some motivation from it. You will either get excited enough to do it or uncomfortable enough to do it. Either way, you are likely to just do it!

5. Finally, you can also use your imagination to motivate you. Think about how you will feel one year from the day you are writing about this, if you do not take any action. Really imagine yourself sitting and journaling about the same issue, the same frustration, the same dissatisfaction.

6. Now, switch to a positive focus. How will you feel if you do take action? Feel the closeness between you and your husband. See yourselves at a fun restaurant enjoying each other.

7. Now decide. What will you do right away to achieve your goals, move closer to your vision, and feel on fire?

Creating a balance of priorities helps you achieve your goals.

With the tendency for motherhood to become all-consuming, it is a challenge for mothers to make the achievement of their goals a priority. Overall, priorities should be the activities that support your core values, goals, and vision.

There is a tendency for mothers to make the family and the children their only priority. But, to feel complete and have an inner fire, you need to have a balance of priorities, both family and personal/individual.

And, of course, there will also be tasks in your life that just don't connect with the higher vision you have for yourself, like being the family chauffeur, for example. Those things need to fit into the balance also.

It helps to understand balance by using the image of a

teeter-totter. You are off balance when one side of the teeter-totter is overloaded and stuck on the ground. To get it moving and balancing properly, you need some things on the other side, too. The teeter-totter is always moving—it goes up and down. Be attentive to the times you are out of balance. Make plans to focus on the other side of the teeter-totter, too.

To help with your balance and to create more positive energy in your life, use your journal to list the things in your day that don't connect with your vision and then brainstorm ways you could make them connect. For example, when you are being a chauffeur, you could listen to books on tape in the car that are for you. Perhaps you could listen to the music list you created earlier that inspires you and makes you happy.

Learn to fit your goals into your life, rather than forcing your life into your goals.

Mothers are weaving a zillion loose threads all the time. You cannot be too rigid about your goals; your life is not that predictable. Instead, you will have to find a way for your goals to fit into your life. No person or program can know what your life is like. Instead, be your own advocate and find ways to have what you want within your life.

For example, when one of my Mothers on Fire partners, Sandra, was a member of a coaching group, she set a goal to compete at a Fitness and Figure Competition. At first, she tried to fit her "mom" and "wife" responsibilities around the traditional bodybuilding program her trainer gave her. For months she struggled. She was consumed with weight training and treadmill work, as well as preparing for, cooking, and eating six meals a day that were separate from her family's meals. She became cranky with the kids when they wouldn't let her work out. She was resentful of her husband who seemed to get time to himself. If she didn't do all the things written down on her program, she felt like a failure and her trainer agreed. He wanted her to train like the "other" people, none of whom were mothers! Even though exercise was her passion, she gave up trying. She decided that she couldn't do it.

After talking about her frustration at one of her monthly coaching meetings, she decided on a different approach. Rather than trying to jam her trainer's program into her already busy life, she created her own program. She decided her goal needed to fit into her life, not her life fitting into her goal.

First, she started to say "no" to some things that were not priorities to her and that she often did because she thought she had to. She thought twice before accepting too many social invitations with people who were only acquaintances. She made sure she didn't "help out" just to be nice or to not disappoint someone. She became more protective of her time and energy. Now she had some breathing room. She did what she could around her training without trying to do it all. If she was at the cottage, she walked and climbed hills, did some light weights and didn't fret about doing it all perfectly. She did what she could with what she had, and she enjoyed herself because she loves working out. (I know— where did she get that gene?)

Her focus shifted onto the positive. I encouraged her to journal at night and only write about what she did that day that she felt good about. There was to be no complaining to anyone, not even to herself in the journal. She wrote down what she ate and what she did for exercise. Whether she lifted weights in the gym or walked the kids to the park, she wrote it down.

Reviewing and focusing on her daily successes, no matter what the size, helped her to believe in herself again and helped her to feel energized and excited about her goal. She started to see progress and that fueled her inner fire even more. She gained confidence and strength by acknowledging what she was doing. This was a huge contrast to feeling bad about everything she wasn't doing.

Instead of getting cranky with the kids, she encouraged them to join her. More than once all three children got on the floor with her as she worked her way through an exercise video. It didn't last long, but it was fun while it lasted. And, of course, the great news was that she was able to sustain her training for over a year and compete as she had hoped. (You can read more about Sandra's story at www.mothersonfire. com.)

Sandra continues to live her vision by making exercise a priority in her life. Many times I'll talk to her in the evening and she'll mention skiing with the kids, or going on bike rides together. Her goals have fit into her life and her kids are enjoying it, too.

Having a Plan B really helps.

Living your vision by setting and achieving goals feels great. It gives you a sense of control over the path and direction of your life. But, being a mother also means plenty of times when your children's needs become the priority no matter how much you plan otherwise. Simply put, if you plan to go to the gym, meet some friends, or finish a project for work and the school calls to report a sick child, your priority will be your child's welfare in that moment.

Moms need to become adept at shifting direction quickly and coming up with a plan B. You just can't be too attached to it all looking a certain way. Being flexible will allow you to find alternative activities or plans when necessary. With a sick child at home, maybe you can do some yoga stretches or forget about exercise that day and spend quiet time reading or writing in your journal as your child sleeps.

The main point is to make sure you find ways to make your own activities a priority, too. One way or another, you will find a way to honor your values and vision, as long as you never give up on yourself. You have a right to be happy and to feel complete and on fire. With your vision as a beacon calling you forward, you will follow it and eventually live like a Mother on Fire.

CHAPTER EIGHT: SUMMARY

✦ The quest for personal fulfillment is about setting goals, but not just any goals, goals that excite you.

- Living a life that is an expression of your authentic self is very powerful.

- Meaningful goals are always connected to your core values, which in turn are connected to your life vision.

- Your life vision is a full-out expression of everything you desire.

- Setting goals helps you become more conscious and active in designing your life.

- Goals can also give your task list more meaning because of how they are connected to your core values.

- Success breeds success.

- Start by setting smaller achievable goals and by taking the path of least resistance.

- Accountability is key to your success.

- Ask a friend or form a group of other moms to hold you accountable to your goals.

- Review your goals regularly to make sure you stay on track.

- In order to feel complete, you must have a balance of both personal and family priorities.

- Fit your goals into your life instead of trying to force your life into your goals.

✦ Don't be too attached to what the journey toward your goal looks like. Be flexible and always have a Plan B in the event your family priorities take over.

✦ You have a right to be happy.

**Find support and create accountability
with other moms at www.mothersonfire.com.**

9

PUTTING LOGS ON YOUR FIRE

I don't believe people are looking for the meaning of life as much as they are looking for the experience of being alive.

—Joseph Campbell, author and mythologist

STEP SIX:
BECOME A MOTHER ON FIRE

What does it feel like to be on fire, to find something you feel passionate about and pursue it? A Grade Five boy explained it perfectly. He was part of a ballroom dancing program that was introduced into New York City public schools in the 1990s. When the interviewer asked this rather awkward, overweight boy why he danced, he replied in earnest and with a sweet naïveté: *Because it makes me feel alive.*

I thought my heart would break with tenderness at such a poignant answer from someone so young. And he was so right. When you find and pursue a passion, you do feel alive.

As we know, mothers weather quite a storm of highs and lows. They don't always feel the positive aliveness that the young boy was talking about. In fact, my clients often talk to me about the emptiness within that hits them occasionally, especially after an exhausting day of ups and downs and meeting everyone else's needs. Or, rather than feeling the joy of feeling alive, they feel the tension of stress.

When people are overloaded, they can go numb. With so many demands on us and so much stimuli, some of us tend to tune out or turn off just to cope. People everywhere are trying to feel alive. Much of consumerism is motivated by that desire. There is often a feeling of excitement, a high, when you purchase that new gadget or spring fashion. The same is true for living on the edge with extreme sports. People feel a rush of adrenaline that makes them feel alive. Luckily, there are many safe ways to feel the pleasure of being alive. One way is to find something you are passionate about and then pursue it. Pursuing a passion is deeply fulfilling. You feel complete—you feel on fire.

What are you passionate about?

In her book, *Finding Your Own North Star*, Life and Career Coach Martha Beck wrote about "Wildly Improbable Goals," or WIGs, for short. For those of you from the business world, you might recognize them as HAGS—Hairy Audacious Goals. One of my mother's groups combined the two into Wildly Audacious Goals or WAGs. Like regular goals, WAGs are connected to your values. What sets them apart is that they are goals that are directly connected to pursuing something you feel passionate about *and* that push you outside of your usual comfort zone. WAGs are like the extreme sport of goal setting; pursuing them really makes you feel alive. Bottom line, they are the logs for your inner fire.

WAGs are meant to push your goal setting out of the ordinary and into the fun and extraordinary. In the Mothers on Fire Coaching Program™, I use them to help clients feel more alive by giving them an extra boost of energy, excitement, and fun.

What are some of your favorite things to do? It could be any activity, like yoga, reading, watching TV, writing, playing ball with your kids, talking with friends, being in nature, or entertaining. Favorite activities often honor your core values and meet many of your needs.

Many of your favorite activities will already be on your vision and goals list. But, to make one into a WAG, you need to push that activity beyond the boundaries of what seems manageable or realistic to something truly wonderful and beyond your wildest dreams. These goals are bigger than the goals you set in Chapter Eight. These goals take you beyond the 10 of your vision and into much larger numbers—like 20 or 50 or even 100 if you can think that big.

If you love watching TV, a WAG might be having a career in television. If you love doing yoga, it might be going on a yoga retreat for three months in India. If you love planning vacations and traveling, you may pursue your passion by starting your own tour company. What are some of your WAGs?

EXERCISE: EXPLORING WILDLY AUDACIOUS GOALS

1. In your journal, write down several activities that you just love, things that make you feel great. They could be anything you love doing—cooking, dancing, lazing around, walking in the woods, playing with your dog, helping others, sitting around the kitchen table talking with friends, volunteering at a women's shelter, singing with your kids, reading the stock market pages, watching TV, etc. You might even find some overlap here with your peak experiences.

2. These are activities for which you feel some passion. Now let's turn up the heat. Take that beloved activity and dream about it. How big can you go? Think about what would make you feel really alive. What would thrill you, but seems improbable, incredible, impossible, and definitely audacious? Here are some examples from clients:

   - Cooking—taking classes at the Cordon Bleu in Paris

   - Dancing—competing at the World Championship Swing Dance competition

   - Playing with the dog—starting a dog rescue organization

   - Volunteering—running a shelter

3. Write your WAGs down in your journal. Create a collage or a vision board if you like. Vision boards tell the story of

your really big goal in pictures, images, and language. Be as creative as you want with this step. Collect pictures and phrases from magazines that reflect your WAGs. Does the idea of pursuing these WAGs excite you? Do they feel a little crazy? Good.

Feel free to set as many WAGs as you want, or just stick to one. It's up to you. One of my clients really loved entertaining friends. In fact, she was passionate about it, but seldom had the time to do it. When I asked her what it would look like if she was to really honor herself and commit to pursuing her passion with a WAG, she suggested that she could entertain more often.

And is that skirting the bounds of possibility? Is that really audacious? I asked.

Well, no, I guess not ... I am passionate about traveling, too. What if I could entertain friends at different and amazing locations all around the world? Would that be a WAG?

Actually, she didn't have to ask that last question because, as she was formulating her really big goal, the log for her fire, the entire climate of the room started to change. She had color in her face. Her heart was starting to race. She became very excited and enamored by the idea of what it would be like to experience it.

That is what we're after. A goal, no matter how "out there," that sparks that level of wonder and excitement in you.

Why WAG?

A mother's day-to-day life can become mundane without her even realizing it. Between the joyful moments of connecting in a loving way with her children, parenting can be a pretty repetitive and tedious job. Just how long can you sit and play house or Tonka toys before you go crazy? The responsibility you feel can be overwhelming, too.

Having a WAG is fun. It can shake you out of your practical rut. One mother I worked with felt envious of the people she saw who were so excited and passionate about things. Nothing really jazzed her. Life was good, she felt she was happy, but she also felt something was missing. So I had her set a WAG. As she was doing it, she kept asking me why.

Why am I doing this if it's so audacious it feels like a fantasy? she inquired several times.

I explained that a WAG is an opportunity to break out of your shell, even if it is just in your head for now. They get you back in touch with a sense of aliveness that spills over into your everyday life.

WAGs are meant to shake you up a bit and get your heart racing. As my client above started to formulate her WAG, which turned out to be a fantasy vacation at a villa somewhere in the Mediterranean, she started to get excited. She started to feel passionate about something. She started to let go a little. She surprised herself. She learned a little more about herself, too. She walked out of the session feeling energized and with a stronger sense of herself.

Learning to dream big and to take those dreams seriously is terribly important for mothers. Along with discovering your values, creating a vision, and setting goals, pursuing something you are truly passionate about is part of reconnecting with yourself on a deep level again and feeling complete.

WAGs often surprise moms. They are not always aware of their big dreams and passions. Sometimes, after doing the WAG exercise, a mother will comment that her WAG was something she had dreamed about when she was younger, or before she had children. Part of the purpose of the WAG exercise is to get back in touch with those dreams, those passions that have been there all along, but have not been set on fire. WAGs contribute to your growing sense of self.

WAGs are goals, too.

As audacious as WAGs are, they are still goals and can be pursued and achieved like any other. Really. I mean it. I have seen my clients achieve their WAGs much to their own amazement. For example, one client, a single parent, loved creating a warm and cozy home for her and her children. She was passionate about homemaking, but it had become a chore and mundane for her. When she broke out of her mental rut and pushed her beloved activity to the bounds of audacity, she saw herself owning her own home. She was currently living with her parents because owning a home seemed completely beyond her financial situation. As well, living with her parents made it difficult to pursue her vision as a contented homemaker.

She became very excited when she started to talk about buying her own place. But then, she just faded as she tried to figure out how to do it.

I am self-employed. Her head dropped. *I'll never get a mortgage.*

We did some coaching together until she was able to let go of her resistance and doubts. Yes, she was self-employed, but she had a consistent part-time professional practice. Owning a home may have seemed incredible, but it wasn't actually impossible. So, instead of focusing on the *how*, I encouraged her to think about the *what*—her dream, her WAG, her new house. We talked about what she wanted it to look like and where she wanted it to be. We also decided on a price that she could afford to spend, which seemed much too low to her. But, we worked on her believing it was possible to find something even in her low price range.

One day, I suggested that, as homework, she talk about this wonderful dream with people who would support her. She went away excited about the idea and for once not worrying about how to make it happen.

Within three days, after talking about her dream to some friends, she had found the name of a mortgage lender who specialized in lending to self-employed people. To her total surprise and relief, she qualified for a mortgage. Now came the task of finding a home in her price range. Again, her coaching helped her to keep a positive focus on the task. So, she started looking. And, lo and behold, she was in her new house just three months after she came up with her WAG.

Don't worry about how you will accomplish your WAG.
Because WAGs are so big, so seemingly improbable, and so
exciting, they can be easily dismissed as impossible to achieve.
If we are not careful, we can get so caught up in the *How is
this going to happen?* perspective that we don't even let a
WAG linger long enough to become a part of us. Many moms
get excited about their WAG only to shut down completely
as soon as they start to think about how to make it happen.

Our inner critic partners with outer circumstances to
throw water on our fire. Throughout the exercises in this
book, you have learned how to recognize your inner critic
and focus more on the positive perspective. This is true with
your WAGs also. You need to tune out the critic and shift
your focus away from the "impossible."

Sometimes, with a WAG, when you really don't have any
idea how to make it happen, you have to just let it go. It is
better to write out the goal and just think about it as something fun than to fret about how to make it happen. By shifting out of the negative focus, surprising things can happen.
For example, the client I mentioned earlier who wanted to
have dinner around the world with her friends had no idea
how to make her WAG a reality, or even if she would try.
But, with coaching, she did get comfortable with the idea
that this was her goal, it represented a rediscovered part of
her, and maybe someday she could enjoy it.

In the meantime, she focused on her other more manageable goals—walking and getting fit. She enrolled in a walking
group and started training to walk a marathon. Soon, a good

friend joined in. As a goal, the group picked a marathon to train for in Big Sur, California. They all registered and trained together.

A little before the big event, another friend got excited and decided to join them. She was already a long distance runner so she knew she could complete the marathon. And so, off they all went. After the race, while they were all sitting to have a celebratory dinner overlooking the ocean, it came to my client suddenly that she was actually living out her WAG! She was overjoyed. The entire experience remains a source of inspiration for her today.

I have seen this happen countless times. When you let go of your resistance to something you really want, it often has a way of developing and becoming a reality. I am reminded of this quote of William Hutchison Murray's from his 1951 book *The Scottish Himalayan Expedition*:

> *Until one is committed, there is hesitancy, the chance to draw back, always ineffectiveness. Concerning all acts of initiative (and creation) there is one elementary truth, the ignorance of which kills countless ideas and splendid plans: that the moment one definitely commits oneself, then Providence moves too. All sorts of things occur to help one that would never otherwise have occurred. A whole stream of events issues from the decision, raising in one's favour all manner of unforeseen incidents and meetings and material assistance, which no man could have dreamed would have come*

his way. I have learned a deep respect for one of Goethe's couplets:

Whatever you can do, or dream you can, begin it!
Boldness has genius, power and magic in it.

The energy and excitement of a WAG is contagious. Talking about your WAG will make you a great role model for your kids as they see you taking your dreams seriously. You become more than just "mom" to them. Because they learn from modeling, they will begin to take their own big dreams seriously as well.

CHAPTER NINE: SUMMARY

✦ Creating Wildly Audacious Goals (WAGs) is meant to push your goal-setting out of the ordinary and into the fun and extraordinary.

✦ WAGs help moms to feel more alive, to feel an extra boost of energy, excitement, and fun.

✦ Part of the purpose of the WAG exercise is to help you get back in touch with those dreams and passions that have been there all along, but have not been set on fire.

✦ WAGs contribute to your growing sense of self.

✦ WAGs can be easily dismissed as impossible to achieve. But, WAGs are like any other goal and you can take steps to achieve them.

✦ When a mom gets excited about pursuing something she is passionate about, her inner critic partners with outer circumstances to throw water on her fire.

✦ You need to tune out the critic and shift your focus.

✦ When you really don't have any idea how to make your WAG happen, you have to just let it go and focus on other goals.

✦ Just setting a WAG and enjoying the idea of it can make a difference in your life.

> **What are some of your favorite things to do?**
> **Share your WAGs on the Mothers on Fire**
> **website forum at www.mothersonfire.com.**

Part Three

A New Beginning

10

KEEPING YOUR
INNER FLAME BURNING

A mighty flame followeth a tiny spark.

—Dante, poet

Congratulations! You have completed the Mothers on Fire Coaching Program™. How do you feel? Are you what my partners and I call a "flaming mama"?

All jokes aside, taking the time to focus and work through the exercises in this book is a major achievement. Give yourself a big pat on the back. Celebrate yourself. Thank yourself for sticking it out. Take a few moments to reflect on how far you have come.

At the start of this book, I asked you if you were living out of the longing of your soul. Since then, you've learned about the ways mothers can lose themselves in motherhood. I also introduced you to a new model of motherhood—the Mother on Fire. You made a commitment to yourself to try. You took stock of your life, found meaning in your needs and emotions, learned about your values, created a vision, wrote out goals, and whipped up a WAG. All these steps helped you to build and burn your inner fire.

After all your self-reflection and hard work, you have arrived at a place that promises a new beginning of sorts. It is no longer a question of whether or not you are living from your soul's desires, the question is *HOW am I living out of the longing of my soul?* Now it is about practicing what you have learned.

Staying connected to your own fulfillment and the joy of being a Mother on Fire is your main focus now. It will require that you pay attention to how you feel and be willing to get back on track often. Nothing travels in a straight line. By keeping your personal fulfillment on your radar screen, you can move forward and back, this way and that, as you continue to find and feel your way to a more joyful and fulfilled life. You will likely need to review some of the steps in this book on occasion. As I mentioned earlier, growth is messy. Things in your life change and you will need to learn to adapt to those changes.

Speaking of your life, I imagine that it looks different to you now from the perspective of being a Mother on Fire. I hope you have discovered a natural energy and contentment that comes from living from your authentic self. Instead of pushing through your life and all its tasks, I hope you are connecting more and more with the energy of your inner fire and letting it move you in the direction of your joy. I truly hope you have found the woman you've always wanted to be and plan on not letting go.

This process of becoming a Mother on Fire is never *really*

finished. You might come upon times when you feel like you are back at Step One. That is natural. But, now you have the tools to navigate your way back to your authentic self and to keep your inner fire burning.

REVISITING THE CHARACTERISTICS OF A MOTHER ON FIRE

1. A Mother on Fire believes she has a right to be happy.

By now you will know that you have the right to be happy, the very first characteristic of being a Mother on Fire. You've understood that happiness is not the automatic result of being a mother. Neither does it come from taking care of everyone else and losing yourself. Rather, it follows from being connected to yourself—specifically, understanding your own needs and knowing you have a right to pursue the fulfillment of them. Happiness comes from appreciating who you are and the elements of your life around you. It is about balancing the demands of being a mother with the choices you continue to make to be your full and complete self. As a Mother on Fire, you now understand how important your own happiness is to the joy of your whole family.

2. A Mother on Fire starts from where she is.

When you looked at your completed Wheel of Life, you faced your life straight on. And, by creating goals for yourself based on your current wheel, you allowed yourself to take charge of your own fulfillment right now, in your life as it is today. No more excuses. You learned that your inner fire existed somewhere within your life at that moment and not in some distant future. You have learned how to work with what you have and not wait until some magic day when all will be right. The longing of your soul is here now, and you have learned to listen and pay attention to it. The wheel you fill out in a year from now will reflect the wonderful steps you've taken today in becoming a Mother on Fire.

3. A Mother on Fire is awake, conscious, and self-aware.
You now have a much stronger sense of yourself. You understand your emotions, needs, and values. It's possible that you went from knowing your family's emotions, needs, and values without knowing your own to a place of self-discovery. You have a connection to your lost goals and dreams and have created some new ones also. Your self-awareness means you are participating more consciously and with more purpose in your life. No more rote activities. You know why you are doing things. No more sleep-walking through your life. You know when your needs are not being met. You also know how to interpret your emotions. You can let yourself feel the longing of your soul because you have the tools to fulfill it. Now that you are on fire, you are a full participant in both creating and participating in your life.

4. A Mother on Fire realizes and accepts that she creates her life.
By completing the exercises in this book, you have demonstrated another characteristic of being a Mother on Fire. You have embraced the idea that you create your life. You no

longer see yourself as a victim of external circumstances or internal limiting beliefs. You now realize you are always in a position of active choice. You can choose to see more than one side of a situation; you can choose to find the positive aspects of your life that will always uplift you. Victimhood is banished as soon as you see that you have options and choices. It all starts with the way you look at things. And, you now look at things from the perspective of being a Mother on Fire.

5. A Mother on Fire is a human BEING.

Through all the exercises in this book, you have learned how to go within and build a more nurturing relationship with yourself. You now catch yourself when you become a human *doing* and slow down to reconnect with yourself. Your inner life, your human *being*, has become important to you. By connecting your activities to your needs and values and even with your WAGs, you feel more fulfilled. When situations or responsibilities threaten to throw water on your inner fire, you protect it. You make sure you keep that flame burning and your relationship to yourself strong. You have made your *being* a priority and your relationships are better for it. You are real with your kids, your partner, your friends, and your family. You are no longer a wind-up toy. You are a real Mother on Fire.

6. A Mother on Fire knows that she is more than "just a mom."

Being a mother is a wonderful and important part of who you are and what you do. Oh, but now you know that there is so much more to you. As a Mother on Fire, you now have an identity that includes all of who you are today and who you hope to become tomorrow. Your life seems bigger and filled with more possibilities. You look for ways to express yourself through friendships, new activities, and in conversations. You are on fire and you are not afraid to let people see it.

7. *A Mother on Fire has focus, vision, and dreams for herself.*

Yes, you still know what your children dream for themselves. And, you know about your partner or spouse's dreams. But, now you also know what *your* dreams are. You have a vision of your life with all its components at a 10. You even have a Wildly Audacious Goal. Having a vision and a dream is the point at which you really feel on fire. It fills you with excitement just thinking about fulfilling them. No matter what the dream, knowing that it is an expression of your authentic self makes it something for you to cherish and work toward. This dream is for you. It is a reflection of your inner fire. It keeps you energized and warm. The fact that pursuing it makes you a great role model for your children is the icing on the cake.

8. *A Mother on Fire takes time to nurture herself.*

As a Mother on Fire, you have learned what it means to take care of yourself. Self-care no longer equals selfishness to you. Rather, it means being at your best. This allows you to be there for others. But, it also means being there for yourself. It means making your emotions, needs, values, goals, and dreams priorities in your life. You have learned how important it is to pay attention to the longing of your soul and to do your best to fulfill it, knowing that what is good for you will benefit your family, too.

9. A Mother on Fire allows herself to be herself.

You can't hide your fire anymore. You are too excited about your life! As a Mother on Fire you have learned to be yourself—the good, the bad, and the ugly! You no longer dismiss your feelings or talk yourself out of expressing your needs. You speak your mind and stand up for yourself if needed. You have likely started to spend time with people who accept you as you are and for who you are. You look for friendships where you can really be yourself. You make an effort to be with people who feel happy for you and your successes, as well as people who are able to listen to your upsets and concerns.

10. A Mother on Fire realizes that she doesn't have to be perfect to be a good enough mother.

Becoming a Mother on Fire means you are letting go of the idea that you need to be perfect to be good enough. You've explored how your striving to be perfect has been a reaction to the opinions and demands of others, including some of the messages of our society. You stop yourself now to see if your thoughts and activities are in alignment with your values. You recognize perfectionism as a false goal. Now you have real and exciting goals that are meaningful and fun to go after. You've started to notice that as you more easily accept yourself, your family benefits, too.

"AND WHAT DO YOU DO?"

One of my inspirations to write this book came from a client of mine who was talking about how to answer that inevitable small-talk question—*And what do you do?* She had just been on a business trip for her husband's work and had encountered that question several times at cocktail parties and other events.

She said she felt herself sink and shrink each time a doctor or a surgeon or a medical expert of some kind asked her. She said she would just shrug and say, *Oh, I'm just a mom.*

When she came back to the coaching group, she was upset by her own inability to recognize and articulate more of who she was and all of what she did.

This question is a difficult one for many people, not just moms. It often feels like the person asking is waiting to judge, ready to decide whether you are worthy of his or her time and attention. It was a great topic for a coaching discussion for mothers because it spoke to everything the group had been working on. It speaks to you, too, the reader, for now that you've completed the Mothers on Fire Coaching Program™, you are not the same person you were when you started.

Now that my client is a Mother on Fire, she answers that age-old question, *So, what do you do?* with a humorous litany of all she does and who she is:

Well, my full-time job is to manage our home and take care of the children. In my spare time, I love to work out and go for bike rides. I guess you could say that exercise is my passion. Also, I planned a great trip to Italy last year and that was amazing. And, I am really committed to my personal growth so I belong to a life-coaching group. I journal and I read. Have you ever read Robin Sharma? I've been reading The Greatness Guide. *Do you know much about that?*

Fully participating in life feels great.

Reconnecting with yourself, living your passion, being a Mother on Fire—these expressions mean the same thing: being a full participant in life, not just an observer from the sidelines. To fully participate in life gives my clients an added purpose and meaning to all the roles they take on. It eliminates some of the boredom that can happen when routines become—well, too routine.

Clients who feel this deepening sense of purpose and fulfillment have more balanced emotional lives. It is as if they have more in reserve for when things get difficult. As one mother said to me, *When I have given to myself, I have so much more to give to others.*

In the personal development field, fulfilling oneself for the sake of fulfilling oneself is reason enough to strive for it. According to personal development philosophy, living your potential is what people are meant to do at whatever level is possible for them. But, for mothers, I have learned that personal fulfillment is not enough on its own, it must benefit their children and their family life in order for it to be a viable and meaningful goal.

That is often the most exciting part of the Mothers on Fire process for my clients. Their own fulfillment blossoms into them becoming a wonderful, positive role model for their children. As moms feel happier, more relaxed, and energized by their lives, their children feel it, too.

In all my years of both counseling and coaching, I have seen this one truth over and over again—of all the things we think children need, what they need the most is their mother to be happy.

Your inner fire is a beacon.

Now that you have become someone whose light is starting to shine in the world openly and without apology, you are contributing to making this world a better place. Your light is not really only about your own fulfillment; rather, it is a beacon that shines a path for all to see.

In a way, becoming a Mother on Fire is like taking a light from your own inner fire and holding it up as a torch for those around you to find their way. In time, some of your inner fire will help to light their torches. As Marianne Williamson wrote in the quote I included in the Introduction, your light illuminates the path for others. It most certainly shines a light for your children.

Endings are also beginnings.

And so, we have come to the end of the book. What an accomplishment—for you and me both! Have you noticed how life moves like a circle? Endings become beginnings as stages are reached, mastered, and used as springboards for further growth.

May your life continue to move and expand and illuminate you with joy, fulfillment, and purpose. Your inner flame will never go out. The energy of your life is always present within you. Whenever you feel it dim, go within and reconnect with it. Let it guide you, fill you with warmth, and light up the way.

And, don't forget, have fun! There is no higher purpose for sacrifice or sorrow. A wise monk once replied to his students who thought he should show more of the reserve and suffering of a singleminded religious follower: "A sad monk is a sad monk."

For you, too: "A sad mom is a sad mom." So, give yourself permission to shine, to feel joy, and to enjoy the process. The world needs your light—it needs your fire.

Chapter Ten: Summary

+ Congratulations! Taking the time to focus and work through the exercises in this book is a major achievement.

+ You have arrived at a new beginning of sorts. Now it's about practicing how to live out of the longing of your heart.

+ Staying connected to your own fulfillment and the joy of being a Mother on Fire is your main focus.

+ Instead of pushing through your life and all its tasks, you are connecting more and more with the energy of your inner fire and letting it move you in the direction of your joy.

+ This process of becoming a Mother on Fire is never *really* finished. But, now you have the tools to navigate your way back to your authentic self and to keep your inner fire burning.

+ You know that you have the right to be happy.

+ You allowed yourself to take charge of your own fulfillment right now, in your life as it is today.

+ You now have a much stronger sense of yourself.

+ You have embraced the idea that you create your life.

+ You have learned how to go within, and build a more nurturing relationship with yourself.

+ You either know or are getting closer to knowing what your dreams are.

+ You have learned what it means to take care of yourself.

+ You can't hide your fire anymore. You are too excited about your life!

+ You are letting go of the idea that you need to be perfect to be good enough.

+ *So, what do you do?* has become a fun question to answer.

✦ Personal fulfillment is not enough on its own; it must benefit your children and your family life in order for it to be a viable and meaningful goal.

Where Do You Go From Here?
Get in Touch and Get Involved

We want you to become a part of building a powerful community of Mothers on Fire. We have seen that when mothers come together in a spirit of self-discovery and support, magic happens.

You can get in touch with us and join our community at www.mothersonfire.com.

Come to the site to:

◆ Get help working through the Mothers on Fire Coaching Program™.

◆ Ask questions.

◆ Provide feedback.

◆ Connect with other moms for support and accountability.

◆ Share your success stories with us.

◆ Read our blogs.

◆ Book us to speak to your group.

✦ Stay connected to all the new ideas and inspirations.

✦ Participate in online discussions.

✦ Attend exciting new teleclasses.

✦ Get lots of great information.

✦ Find out what's new.

See you there:
www.mothersonfire.com

BIBLIOGRAPHY

Marano, Hara Estroff. *A Nation of Wimps*. New York: Broadway Books, 2008.

Branden, Nathaniel. *The Psychology of Self-esteem: A Revolutionary Approach to Self-Understanding that Launched a New Era in Modern Psychology*. New York: Jossey-Bass edition, 2001.

Carson, Richard D. *Taming Your Gremlin: A Guide to Enjoying Yourself*. New York: HarperPerennial, 1990.

Center for Nonviolent Communication. *Needs List*. 2009. www.cnvc.org. Email: cnvc@cnvc.org Phone: +1.505-244-4041

Maslow, Abraham. *The Farther Reaches of Human Nature*. New York: Viking Press, 1971.

Murray, William Hutchinson: *The Scottish Himalayan Expedition*. London: J.M. Dent & Sons Ltd, 1951.

Sharma, Robin. *The Greatness Guide: Powerful Secrets for Getting to World Class*. New York: HaperCollins, 2008.

Tolle, Eckhart. *A New Earth: Awakening to Your Life's Purpose*. New York: Plume, 2006

_____. *The Power of Now: A Guide to Spiritual Enlightenment*. Vancouver, Canada: Namaste Publishing Inc and Novato, Calif.: New World Library, 2004

Beck, Martha: *Finding Your Own North Star: Claiming the Life You Were Meant to Live.* New York: Three Rivers Press, 2001.

Rosenfeld, Alvin, M.D, and Wise, Nicole. *The Over-Scheduled Child: Avoiding the Hyper-Parenting Trap.* New York: St. Martin's Press, 2000.

Williamson, Marianne. *A Return to Love: Reflections on the Principles of A Course in Miracles.* New York: Harper-Collins, 1992.

INDEX

needs (*continued*)
    list of needs, 79–81
    personal needs, 11, 19, 26, 30,
        35, 36, 79, 82–83, 84–86, 90,
        147
        leading to what you want,
            84–86, 149
        learning to express, 151
        reconnecting with your
            needs, 75–76, 147
    taking care of others' needs,
        20, 23, 26, 31, 83, 113, 127, 132
    understanding their message,
        148
    wants and needs, 19, 23, 24, 30,
        35, 37, 93, 94
needy vs. needs, 81–82
negative self-talk, 49–50, 62, 139
    affecting emotions, 86–87
    journaling as a way to manage,
        50–51
    switching from negative to
        positive focus, 62–64, 139
New Earth, A (Tolle), 101
nurturing, 23, 103
    nurturing self, 38, 39, 69, 149,
        150–51

obligations, 19, 24, 76, 113
obstacles to change, overcoming,
    43–56, 76
    journaling as a tool, 47–48
Oprah (TV show), 2
over-achievement, 17
over-compensation, 22
over-functioning, 21–25, 31, 38
over-identifying as a mom, 4, 17
over-parenting, 18, 24–25, 95–97

passion, 19
    as a basis for Mothers on Fire
        Coaching Program, 131–32

passion (*continued*)
    finding inner passion, 7, 13
    fire as symbol of, 6
    need to live a passionate life, 2,
        13, 20–21, 36, 119, 153
    reconnecting with, 11, 30, 50,
        64, 137, 153
    and setting Wildly Audacious
        Goals, 133, 134–35, 136, 137
peak experience, 98–99
    and core values, 98–99
    and values clarification, 99–105
people-pleasing, 29–31
perfectionism, 14, 24
    leading to guilt, 27
    Mother on Fire not needing to
        be perfect, 40, 151
personal fulfillment, 36, 56–57,
    145–46, 147–48, 153–54, 155.
    See also full life
    benefits of fulfilling longing of
        your soul, 31–32, 48, 50, 55,
        145–46
    creating own life, 37–38, 149
    not having because of guilt,
        19–20
    personal responsibility for
        creating, 37–38, 148–49
personal needs, 11, 19, 26, 30, 35, 36,
    79, 82–83, 84–86, 90, 147. *See also*
    needs
    leading to what you want,
        84–86, 149
    learning to express, 151
    reconnecting with your needs,
        75–76, 147
"Phenomenal Woman" (song), 61
plan B, 124–26
pleasing others rather than self,
    29–31
positive focus, 76–77, 105, 123–24,
    126, 138

169

ACKNOWLEDGMENTS

I finally understand why artists spend so much time thanking people when they get on stage to accept their awards. The list is long of all the influences that converge to make something happen. Writing this book is no different. I will, however, not thank my childhood ballet teacher. Instead, I have mentioned here the people who have had a more direct effect on the writing and completion of this project. And to each and every one, I am deeply appreciative.

To my clients, the amazing mothers who have shown much courage and trust, I thank you for your openness and participation in making the most of this one and precious life you were given.

To my business partners and dear friends, Sandra De Tina and Renée Walker. Life would be less vibrant, meaningful or fun without you. Thank you for being in my life. I cherish you both.

To my colleagues and owners JP Pawliw-Fry, Bill Benjamin and Elizabeth Pawliw-Fry at the Institute for Health and Human Potential (IHHP). I could not have done this without your faith in me. You have helped me grow my confidence and provided me with countless wonderful opportunities. I am proud of the work we do together and honored to be making such a difference in people's lives.

To George Foster and Sara Patton, who showed patience along with their talent to bring this book to life.

To Gwen Robinson, for your good eyes and warm heart. I would surely go crazy without your professional skills.

To Yasemin Ucar, my editor. Without you, I only had a lot of ideas and a willingness to persevere. You made me into a writer. You are the editor of my dreams. Here's to many more books together, if you can stand it!

ABOUT THE AUTHOR

Lisa Garber has been coaching women's groups for over ten years and is a passionate advocate for mothers living their full potential. Lisa is a Certified Professional Co-active Coach, a psychotherapist, and an author of transformational books and programs. She was one of the first life coaches in Canada, starting her practice in 1997. She was a professor of counseling psychology at George Brown College, developed the first women's-only treatment program for addiction at the Donwood Institute, and is currently the Director of Coaching at The Institute for Health and Human Potential, an international training company in emotional intelligence for leaders. She holds a Masters degree in Counseling Psychology from the University of Toronto and is a partner and resident expert for Mothers on Fire Inc.

Lisa knows first hand what it is like to transform your life. At the age of sixteen, she left school to pursue her dream of becoming a professional singer. She performed in clubs all over North America. She appeared on numerous radio and television shows, including a live concert at Camp Fortune Canada for over ten thousand fans. Lisa has sung background vocals on records for artists such as Art Garfunkle and Bette

Midler. She also had an international publishing contract and was well respected as a song writer.

But when her musical career no longer fulfilled her, Lisa took the brave step of retiring at the age of thirty-three and going back to school. As a high-school dropout, university was both scary and exciting. Yet she persevered and thrived. Helping people fulfill themselves has become Lisa's passion. She knows how hard it can be, and she knows it is worth it.

About Mothers on Fire Inc.

After being part of a life-coaching group for many years, Renée Walker and Sandra De Tina wanted to share their exciting journey of self-discovery with other mothers.

They noticed that many "mummy" companies tended to recognize mothers as mothers only and neglected them as individuals. On the other hand, most personal development companies focused only on the individual and tended to ignore the reality of what it's like to be a mother. Mothers on Fire was created to bridge that gap.

Visit us at www.mothersonfire.com for all the latest exciting news, articles, and events that Mothers on Fire Inc. is offering.

.

LaVergne, TN USA
11 January 2011
212026LV00008B/14/P